Shayne Wheeler is a pastor who refuses to allow theology to get in the way of ministry. Anyone who knows Shayne knows he exemplifies the subtitle of this excellent book. He has indeed followed Jesus into the thorny places. Before you finish the first chapter, you will be inspired to do the same!

ANDY STANLEY
Founder, North Point Ministries

Following Christ can be a messy and challenging journey because we often find ourselves in prickly and confusing places with the most unlikely people. *The Briarpatch Gospel* provides a window into Shayne Wheeler's piece of the patch, and an invitation to jump on in and join the adventure. This is not about playing it safe or seeing the purpose of life as merely being nice and doing a little good here and there. This is about taking God and God's world seriously—and it's how I want to live.

STEPHEN A. HAYNER
President, Columbia Theological Seminary

Shayne Wheeler ministers not in the safe (but shrinking) enclaves of the traditional and the conservative, but instead within the progressive, secular, post-Christian culture. This book is the distillation of many encounters Shayne has had with people in his neighborhood. All readers who want to do the same kind of ministry can learn much from overhearing these conversations. And those who do such work will also find encouragement here when they are criticized by both the hostile skeptical and the hostile devout.

TIM KELLER
Redeemer Presbyterian Church, New York City

In *The Briarpatch Gospel*, Shayne Wheeler takes us on a journey underneath the superficiality present in much of American Christianity. It's a raw and honest invitation to face the dark, uncertain, and thorny places of our lives, along with a promise that Jesus is already there—waiting for us.

DANNY WUERFFEL
Heisman Trophy winner and executive director of
Desire Street Ministries

Shayne Wheeler's narrative of how his church learned to follow Christ into areas of fear and challenge—"the briarpatch"—is just what the doctor ordered. I was personally challenged to new depths of honesty and faithfulness in ways I did not expect. Bravo for a book that deeply connects a theology of missional identity, and our unique Christ-centered calling, with the rise of the post-Christendom generation.

JOHN H. ARMSTRONG
President, ACT 3, and author of *Your Church Is Too Small*

As the messy edges of morality fray and the ever-stretching boundaries of our Christian consciousness expand, there is an urgent need for clarity in conviction and theological dialogue around today's most pressing concerns. Honest, pastoral, confessional, and prophetic, Shayne Wheeler courageously brings his readers into these murky waters. *The Briarpatch Gospel* is fresh and timely, an important contribution to the emerging conversations of our Christian identity and what compels us to engage today's greatest human needs.

CHRISTOPHER L. HEUERTZ
Author of *Unexpected Gifts: Discovering the Way of Community*

Shayne Wheeler writes like he preaches—earthy and edgy—just enough to make the religious people nervous and the irreligious interested. This dispatch from the briarpatch is a provocative book for both, a page-turning debut filled with wisdom and encouragement.

SCOT SHERMAN
President, Newbigin House of Studies

This unusual book has thrilled me afresh with the sheer magnitude of what God has done in Christ. (And I've been around a long time.) Shayne Wheeler is a rare combination of one with a profound understanding of the New Testament message, irrepressible storytelling, and a mischievous sense of humor; but in all he exalts the grace and love of God. He is an artist with words, with a wealth of literary resources. But what gives this work depth is that he has suffered, and so runs deep. Read this book and be transformed.

ROBERT THORNTON HENDERSON
Author of *The Church and the Relentless Darkness*

The Briarpatch Gospel is a conversation igniter for real people with real questions about the most tension-filled topics holding people back from true faith. I recommend it to anyone who wants to move past shallow talk and dig deep into the messiness of love and community.

JEFF SHINABARGER
Founder, Plywood People, and author of *More or Less: Choosing a Lifestyle of Excessive Generosity*

Too often, the church has offered false sanctuary behind walls of greeting-card platitudes, pretty buildings, tidy self-help programs, and pat answers. Shayne Wheeler shows us the uncomfortable truth that Jesus is calling us to come out from behind the walls we build and join him in the briarpatches of the world, where he delights to meet us. Do we really trust Jesus enough to follow him into the thickets of life? Will we move toward the pain, or flee from it? Is the briarpatch the place for you? Yes, if you will trust and go. Shayne offers an encouragement: You don't journey there alone. He has stumbled into the dark tangle of thorns, and he knows—it's the only way to really meet Jesus and his family.

RAY CANNATA
Senior pastor, Redeemer Presbyterian Church of New Orleans

I am thankful for *The Briarpatch Gospel*. Wheeler writes with depth and simplicity, transparency and humor in describing God's disruptive grace. He tells his own story in a way that embraces skeptics and strugglers as he invites us into a beautifully woven narrative that compels us to keep reading until finished, while being nourished all along the way. We will use this book in our church in the years to come, and I will count it among my favorites.

MIKE KHANDJIAN
Senior pastor, Chapelgate Presbyterian Church, Greater Baltimore, Maryland

Shayne Wheeler tackles the messier issues of life head-on because he knows it's in life's messiness that we find God, and it's in the broken places where we find God's healing. *The Briarpatch Gospel* reminds us that Christianity was never meant to be a religion of safety and comfort and that God calls us to carry our light into the darkest shadows where it can actually be of use. We don't have to fear the hard questions, even if we don't always know the answers.

JOSH JACKSON
Cofounder and editor in chief, *Paste* magazine

THE BRIARPATCH GOSPEL

THE

BRIARPATCH

GOSPEL

FEARLESSLY FOLLOWING JESUS

INTO THE THORNY PLACES

SHAYNE

WHEELER

TYNDALE
MOMENTUM

An Imprint of
Tyndale House
Publishers, Inc.

Visit Tyndale online at www.tyndale.com.

Visit Tyndale Momentum online at www.tyndalemomentum.com.

TYNDALE is a registered trademark of Tyndale House Publishers, Inc. *Tyndale Momentum* and the Tyndale Momentum logo are trademarks of Tyndale House Publishers, Inc. Tyndale Momentum is an imprint of Tyndale House Publishers, Inc.

The Briarpatch Gospel: Fearlessly Following Jesus into the Thorny Places

Designed by Dean H. Renninger

Edited by Dave Lindstedt

Published in association with Ambassador Literary Agency, Nashville, TN 37205.

The stories in *The Briarpatch Gospel* are true, but names and other identifying details have been changed to safeguard the privacy of the individuals involved.

Library of Congress Cataloging-in-Publication Data

Wheeler, Shayne.
   The briarpatch Gospel : fearlessly following Jesus into the thorny places / Shayne Wheeler.
      p. cm.
   Includes bibliographical references.
   ISBN 978-1-4143-7230-3 (pbk.)
1. Christian life. I. Title.
   BV4501.3.W45 2013
   248.4—dc23   2012028871

Printed in the United States of America

19	18	17	16	15	14	13
7	6	5	4	3	2	1

To Carrie,

for taking with me the road less traveled.

You have made all the difference.

CONTENTS

INTO THE BRIARPATCH

TRANSFORMING THE BRIARPATCH

THE PROBLEM OF
THE BRIARPATCH

CHAPTER 1

YOU ARE HERE
COMING TO GRIPS WITH OUR FEAR

A ship is safe in harbor, but that's
not what ships are for.
WILLIAM SHEDD

A dead thing can go with the stream,
but only a living thing can go against it.
G. K. CHESTERTON

I was three weeks out of seminary and working as a youth
pastor in Virginia when I first went to New York City, leading
a mission trip to hand out gospel tracts in Brighton Beach,
near Coney Island in Brooklyn. We were an idealistic group,
convinced that our finely crafted leaflets had the potential
to reach hundreds, if not thousands, of hard-hearted New
Yorkers for Christ. We had ten thousand tracts, so our goals
for transforming lives and changing hearts wouldn't exactly
measure up to Billy Graham's famous sixteen-week revival
in 1957, when millions heard the gospel at Madison Square
Garden, Yankee Stadium, and Times Square. Still, we figured
that a few thousand conversions would suffice.

Within hours, my high-flying dream of evangelistic star-dom had begun to stall as, one after another, the disinterested denizens of Brighton Beach accepted one of our tracts, gave it a quick glance, and dropped it without even breaking stride. The discarded leaflets began to pile up in the trash cans and blow like forsaken tumbleweeds on the streets of this bustling city. Rather than capturing a city for Christ, we were creating more work for the New York City sanitation workers. By the end of the day, my evangelistic fervor was in a steep death spiral.

Welcome to earth, Shayne. I hope you enjoyed your flight.

By the third day, embarrassment had given way to a growing cynicism. We decided to move our team out to the famous boardwalk, where folks would presumably be more jovial, friendly, and open to our efforts.

This was not a good move.

The unrepentant littering continued. One young member of our team approached two men who may have been members of the Russian mafia. After treating him to a litany of profanity and threats, one of the men pulled back his jacket to reveal a holstered handgun, not so politely inviting our teenager to walk away and not return.

Things were not going as planned.

Disillusioned, I stopped near a bench overlooking the ocean, where an elderly gentleman in a well-worn fedora sat watching the waves, a wooden cane hooked on the backrest. Judging him unlikely to be hiding a gun under his faded green summer jacket, I sat down to lick my wounds.

A saline breeze had begun to move onshore. "Rain is com-ing," he said in heavily accented English.

"Uh-huh," I replied.

"What brings you to boardwalk?"

"These stupid tracts."

"What are they about?"

"Jesus," I muttered.

"You think Jesus is stupid?"

"We've handed out thousands of these, and most have ended up on the ground. It feels no different than if they were restaurant coupons or flyers for one of the strip clubs."

"Yes. Everybody is selling something," the man agreed. "But if your Jesus is so important to you Christians, why do you make us read? You say he lives in you—so why you don't show him to us?"

"What do you mean?" I asked.

"You give me piece of paper that says your belief about Jesus, but you don't know me. Why don't you want to know me? A paper is just paper. Your paper is no different than other piece of paper, so why should I read a paper from a stranger? If you are Christian and Jesus is in you like you say, do not bother me with paper. Do not be stranger."

"Okay," I replied, uncertain of what to say next.

"Hello. I am Ilya," he said, holding out his hand. "From Russia."

I had a feeling he was going to teach me a thing or two about Jesus, and I wasn't sure I was going to like it. Control is not something I surrender easily.

"I'm Shayne, from . . . well, I guess I am from Virginia now."

Having emigrated from Russia many decades before, Ilya

had raised his family in the eclectic, crowded neighborhood of Brighton Beach. We talked for more than two hours— about family and grandkids, retirement, health, neighbors, and our wives. We talked about Jesus, too. Ilya was Jewish and had heard a lot about Jesus over the course of more years than I had been alive. He had lots of questions, some of which I could answer. Many I could not, despite my advanced theological degree.

I had never had such a muddled, or meaningful, discussion about Jesus. My seminary answers often sounded platitudinous and even hollow. Yet as Ilya and I talked, Jesus was there, sitting with us in the pregnant pauses and cul-de-sacs that littered our conversation. He had never been more present and alive to me, and I found myself wishing I knew him better.

"Rain is here," Ilya said as he raised his eyes to the gathered clouds. "I must go. We both have much to think about. Getting to know you made your Jesus more real to me, and I thank you. Good-bye, friend." He tipped his fedora and was gone.

Who knows what ever became of that conversation in Ilya's life, but I knew something had changed in me.

I had traveled all the way from Virginia to Brighton Beach, ostensibly to introduce people to Jesus—to change their lives by means of a carefully worded and expertly designed pamphlet—but it seemed that I was the one who needed the introduction, or at least a reunion.

I first met Jesus when I was in college, through a group of people who loved and cared for one another in a way I didn't know was possible. Jocks and jesters, nerds and rebels, I found them to be a weird Breakfast Club community of true friendship and affection, held together by their common identity as Christians. It was weird. *They* were weird. But I was intrigued.

They called themselves the Fellowship of Christian Athletes, and they met on Thursday evenings in the basement of one of the dorms. The friend who invited me said that only a few were actually athletes, and you didn't even have to be a Christian to come. Nevertheless, I quickly realized that Jesus was real to this diverse gathering of college students—not in a creepy, cultish, one-dimensional way, but something deeper, like it made them better people, more peaceful and kind and full of joy. The life of Jesus just seemed to be in them, and I gradually absorbed that life into my own.

At the time, I couldn't have given an account for the theological basis of sin, repentance, or substitutionary atonement. I would have stuttered cross-eyed if you had asked me about the factual truth of the Resurrection or the reality of the Trinity, but I knew Jesus and I knew he had changed me. I knew that God had spoken his benediction of grace over me—that he had welcomed me into his family, warts and all, and called me his own. I knew that, through Jesus, God hadn't just forgiven me, he also loved me like his own child. This was easy for me to accept because my father had always loved and accepted me, even though I wasn't perfect and often needed correction. I knew that nothing could cause my dad to stop loving me, and now I knew I had the same kind of love from God. It was real. Palpable. I could feel it in my bones.

Yet here I was, eight years later, on the streets of Brooklyn, relying more on propositions and formulas, slogans, and thinly veiled intimidation—"God will get you in the end if you don't straighten up and get right with Jesus"—to try to get people's attention. Jesus had become more of a ticket out of hell than an invitation into a rich and loving life with God. What happened to the life and the joy, the simplicity of knowing that Christ was living in me? I had fancied myself as brave and bold to venture into big, bad Brooklyn, armed with theologically sound literature. But that wasn't courage; it was cowardice. I was hiding behind my pamphlets and the impersonal anonymity of the big city, afraid to let the Jesus within me breathe and be seen, simple and unadorned.

As I hoisted my backpack onto my shoulders, the tracts that now weighed me down seemed unloving and cruel. As awkward and unprepared as I had felt while talking to Ilya, I realized that our conversation had at least been *real*. And I hadn't even shown him one of my flyers. With a newfound determination, I resolved that never again would I hide behind my fear of not having all the answers or pretend to know more than I do. That day at the boardwalk was my first step away from cowardice and my first step toward a journey that would lead me into a vast and unpredictable briarpatch of questions, doubts, and fears, of untidy relationships and heartbreaking stories.

If we're honest, we want things to be easy in our relationship with God, and especially in our relationships at church.

But it just doesn't work that way. Church, for many of us, is a place where real problems and struggles are covered in a veneer of genteel seersucker or khaki. Polite, superficial smiles mask the silent screams of struggle and pain because Sunday morning is just not the time or place to deal with the carnage of life—especially a life that has gone badly off the rails. But if the truth be told, the stories of the Bible can feel as lifeless and two-dimensional as a flannel storyboard, irrelevant to what we are experiencing in our fractured families, broken bodies, or emaciated souls. Nobody questions the blatant contradiction between our Sunday school façades and the inner turmoil of our fears and doubts. We would rather streak naked down the center aisle than ever confess that we sometimes question whether God is even real. Sound familiar? Welcome to the briarpatch. You are not weird. And life with Jesus will not make all your problems vanish.

The unfortunate reality is that we often feel more comfortable—more alive—at the local pub than at a church potluck, and it sometimes seems far more likely that we will run into Jesus downtown than at church. The image of Jesus being confined to an hour on Sunday morning or in a room politely fitted with matching pews (or padded chairs) and carpet, under outdated brass chandeliers and anchored with a pipe organ (or a stage for the band) just doesn't seem to match how the Son of God is portrayed in the Bible. Sure, he was a regular attender at synagogue, but he did some of his best work in the public places—at parties, with his friends, in the public square, among whores and crooks. And he probably didn't bathe very often. His life on earth was messy, and it ended brutally, on the cross, with a prickly crown of thorns pressed into his brow. Maybe he was trying to tell us something there. Perhaps that life is going to be unavoidably prickly and painful?

The gospel tracts were just one of the ways I had avoided wading into the thicket. I was certain there were others. Almost imperceptibly, my heart had been locked securely behind the gates of systematic theology and pat Sunday school answers, far from the real-time doubt and disillusionment of the people around me—far from the place where Jesus delights to meet us. In playing it safe, I had almost missed getting to know Jesus.

I realized that Jesus is in the midst of that jumbled thicket—the briarpatch—waiting for me to venture in. He's waiting for you, too. And if we follow him, we will find him. If we have the courage to enter the briarpatch, we will discover that Jesus is real and that his life, death, and resurrection matter—not just in the afterlife, but now. Here. In this place that he created, loves, and is renewing. We will discover that our lives matter—to the homeless man on the corner begging for a quarter, the bald lady at church going through chemo for the second time, or the gay man who loves Jesus but has been rejected by Christians so many times that he has finally given up trying. This is life in the briarpatch.

To be sure, the briarpatch is not for the faint of heart. There are risks involved. We will be shunned, even criticized, by the keepers of the Christian status quo. They will not appreciate the questions we ask, much less the answers (or lack of answers) we offer.

IS THE BRIARPATCH CALLING YOU?

Is the briarpatch where Jesus makes his home for you? If you are a Christian, the answer is yes. Your calling as a follower of Jesus is to do just that . . . follow! Jesus can, of course, be found in the sanctuary, but his presence is not limited to a scheduled hour between breakfast and lunch on Sunday morning. He *sends* us—tells us to "go into the world" in his name—and promises to be with us to the very end. Furthermore, he is revealed in the pages of the Bible and meets us in prayer. Reading the Scriptures and praying regularly are essential for all followers of Christ, and a journey into the briarpatch assumes that worship and study and prayer are vital and vibrant parts of your life. If not, believe me, walking with Jesus among the thorns and thistles will renew a desire and need for these things! But the point is, your spiritual life will be anemic without both. We meet Jesus in corporate worship and personal prayer, but we follow him into the briarpatch every day to bring love and healing to our world.

But what if you are not a Christian, or have long ago decided that Christianity is just not for you? Perhaps you have had your fill of boring, perfunctory songs and prayers. You just cannot stomach the churches full of some of the most self-centered, hypocritical bipeds who have ever lumbered across the earth. If this is what it means to be a Christian, you'll pass.

If that is you, there is hope. Real hope. Don't give up. All I ask is that you join me in the briarpatch and just see if you don't find the Jesus of the Bible—the real one, who loved prostitutes, hypocrites, and thieves. The one who hung out with the poor, the marginalized, and the disenfranchised. The one who railed against corruption, greed, suffering, and injustice. The one who invited *everyone* to come and find hope, meaning, and the life of God in him—without becoming myopic, self-righteous, religious fanatics.

This is the Jesus who made this world and called it "good." But what he made has fallen into disrepair and is often overrun with the brambles of suffering, sin, alienation, and shallow religiosity. The list could go on and on. But if Jesus is really the Redeemer he claims to be, he is not done with you and me, and he is not done with the world—as broken as it may be. He has come to rescue and restore, to bring healing and hope. He has come to put the world to rights, to clear away the brush and the brambles and restore things to how they were always supposed to be. Not only is he doing this, he invites us to join him.

But how?

It just seems too difficult and way too scary at times. So we settle for memory verses, "quiet times," potlucks, and sermons no longer than thirty minutes. I guess it's just easier that way. But what if we had the courage to follow Jesus into the thicket of his healing grace?

WELCOME TO THE BRIARPATCH

Sarah was new to Atlanta and had recently endured a hard breakup with her boyfriend. She had no friends in the city, was under tremendous stress in her new job, and quickly spiraled into a severe depression. Having grown up in church, Sarah could not remember a time when Jesus wasn't real to her—near and intimate. But now he seemed to have been swept away in the vortex of sadness that sucked all the joy out of her life.

She was in trouble, but admitting to such a desperate depression was terrifying. Christians are supposed to be happy, right? They are supposed to have faith and joy and hope. But all the memory verses now failed her and she couldn't muster the strength to pray.

She approached me one Sunday and simply said, "I think I need to talk to someone."

When Sarah told me her story, it was clear we were going into the briarpatch of her spiritual and emotional suffocation—a place of darkness where the birds no longer sing, the sun no longer shines, and God no longer cares. If you have ever loved someone who was enduring a season of depression—or been there yourself—you understand that it is more than just having "the blues." It is the "Dementor's Kiss" that can "drain peace, hope, and happiness out of the air" around you.[1] The nearer we draw to someone whose soul is struggling to breathe, the thinner the air becomes for us as well. But draw near we must.

After listening patiently to Sarah, I said, "I know it feels as if someone has put a blanket over your soul and God has turned his back on you. I've had times like that myself. But," I assured her, "God has not gone anywhere. He is with you. You will get through this, but you might need others to believe for you when you don't have the strength on your own."

She gave a slight nod, but her expression said, *Yeah, yeah. I hear what you're saying, but it's just not working for me.*

"Come with me for a minute," I said. "I want you to meet someone."

I introduced Sarah to a woman who I knew would understand; someone who had been to the depths and back, someone with whom she could open up without fear of rejection or judgment. Over time, Sarah was invited to a community group of people her own age. She established some good friendships with people who loved her, prayed with her, and studied the Scriptures with her, even though she often wasn't much fun to be around.

A few weeks ago, when Sarah came forward for Communion, there was something different about her. She was smiling. The circumstances of her life hadn't changed a whole lot, but the thorns of her depression had not kept a group of ordinary Christians from loving her. As they engaged with Sarah in the briarpatch, Jesus had met them there. And the touch of his Spirit was evident.

Invitations into the briarpatch happen in all different ways and come in all shapes and sizes.

I met Charlie a few months ago, when he came to All Souls for the first time. I happened to walk past him just after the service ended, so I stopped and said hello. The fear that shot through his body when the preacher stopped to talk to him was almost visible. He seemed certain that the inquisition was about to begin.

Within five minutes, I learned that he had believed in Jesus longer than I had and was new to town. He didn't know anyone and was nervous about his new job. He also fully expected that we would not want him in our church. It took a great deal of courage for him to let down his guard, especially so quickly. But that's just what he did.

"See, Pastor, I'm one of those boys who likes to kiss other boys."

I tried to hold it together, but I just couldn't. "Wow!" I said as I began to laugh. "Is that how you tell people you're gay? I've heard it said a lot of ways, but that's a new one!"

He squirmed and let out a nervous laugh, and I could tell he was just waiting for me to ask some uncomfortable questions—was he celibate? did he have a boyfriend? had he read Leviticus?—and then explain why he wouldn't be welcome at our church unless he changed his ways. It was pretty clear he expected judgment and rejection.

Instead, I looked him in the eye and said, "If you are a follower of Christ, you're my brother, and you're welcome here either way. I'm guessing I don't need to tell you what the Bible says about homosexuality because you probably know better than I do. But your being gay doesn't put you into some special category of sinner. It just means you struggle to follow Jesus, just like I do. You and I both are called to conform our lives to the righteousness of Christ, and you and I are both going to fail miserably at times. But I am willing to walk down that road with you for as long as it takes. And I want you to walk down my roads with me. As Christians, we are called to enter together into the mess and the mystery of following Jesus."

He was speechless. It may have been my cologne.

Finally, he muttered, "Okay."

"I need coffee," I said, pointing toward our lobby. "Want some?"

I don't pretend to understand what it's like to be a gay Christian.* But it's not necessary for me to understand in order to give my friendship to Charlie, any more than he needs to know my sins and doubts before deciding to be my friend. We don't have to have all the answers. We don't even have to agree on the questions. Following Jesus means only that we have the courage to love as he did, even when we don't understand.

When Jesus went to the homes of tax collectors, and when he associated with adulterers, prostitutes, lepers, and Samaritans, he was misunderstood and reviled—the religious leaders called him "a friend of sinners" (Matthew 11:19).

Was Jesus compromising the truth when he ate with tax collectors and sinners? No, he was demonstrating his love for them. And the one truth that really mattered—the same truth that matters in our day as well—is that we're all lost sinners in need of redemption, which comes only through the sacrificial death and resurrection of Jesus. Our calling is to love other people as Christ has loved us (that is, while we were yet sinners), and allow the Holy Spirit to "convict the world of its sin, and . . . guide [us] into all truth" (John 16:8, 13, NLT).

The fact of the matter is that it would be much easier if there were no gays or liberals or divorced people or pagans at our church. It's awkward to meet a woman in church who used to be a man and try to figure out if you should refer to her (him) as "he" or "she." It would be much easier to avoid it altogether, ignore her and silently hope she decides to go

---

* Some people believe that the term "gay Christian" is an oxymoron—that it's not possible to be both gay and Christian. But if the blood of Christ doesn't extend to *everyone* who calls on the name of the Lord, how can we say it covers *us* in our own fallenness?

to another church. Then again, it seems as if that would be like avoiding Jesus, too.

I saw Charlie again two weeks later. Fifth row, right on the center aisle. And he had brought his grandma with him.

Welcome to the briarpatch, Charlie.

YOU ARE HERE

I am certainly no titan of the faith, and I don't want you to think you have to be a Christian superhero in order to walk through the briarpatch. All you need is the courage to be yourself—the geek who has a gift for numbers and a passion for science fiction; the mom who considers it a success just to survive (without anyone getting hurt) until the kids go to bed; the executive who has been wounded by the church and wrestles with serious doubts, but can't get over the beauty of Jesus.

All you need is the courage to believe that God knew what he was doing when he made you, with all of your quirks, passions, idiosyncrasies, and general stupidity, and to extend the same faith, hope, and love to your friends and neighbors.

All you need is the courage to believe that your life matters to God—the way you befriend your neighbor who has just been diagnosed with cancer or listen to your coworker going through a divorce; the way you patiently love your teenager and hope for his or her eventual return to the human race, or struggle to forgive one of the many people who have wronged you. Such actions of grace and affection are the stuff of redemption.

All you need is the courage to acknowledge that life—your

life—really stinks sometimes and seems to oscillate between crisis and boredom and back again. They may never make a Lifetime movie about your life, but you are already living in the briarpatch, and this is where Jesus delights to meet you.

In the pages that follow, I will share some of my own experiences of the tragedy and tedium of life. And you may have your own stories that are far more acute and wearisome than mine. But here's the point: The briarpatch is where God shows up. It's where we meet Jesus. Somewhere along the way, we have bought into the idea that we must go to a particular place or through a ritualized routine in order to find God.

I certainly affirm the power and necessity of meeting God in corporate worship and pursuing him in private prayer, but what do you do when you just can't find the strength? What do you do when your path has been a protracted series of disappointment, disillusionment, and despair? Or when you're on a path full of sickness, betrayal, and loneliness, and the thought of mustering the spiritual or emotional energy to pursue Jesus seems impossible, like reaching the summit of Mount Everest—when you are out of shape, out of gas, and out of breath, wishing someone were waiting with a tank of oxygen to help you up this insurmountable religious peak, or you are paralyzed with the fear of slipping and falling into the dark crevasses on either side of you. Truth be told, you can't take another step, much less make it to the summit in hopes of experiencing the transcendent presence of God.

I have good news for you. Jesus isn't only on the summit. He's also in the deep valleys, on the windswept slopes, and in the cavernous crevasses. He's in the seemingly dark places of your exhaustion and confusion. He's in the briarpatch, amid all the tangle, thorns, and confusion, and it's where he does some of his best work.

But what does that look like?

We expect encounters with the living God to be earth-shattering, but it wasn't that way (at least initially) for most of the people who met Jesus after he was raised from the dead. His disciples were having a despondent dinner, and Jesus walked in and asked for something to eat (Luke 24:35-43). Another time, they were having a really bad day at work, until Jesus arrived and showed them a better way (John 21:1-11). On a third occasion, two men were walking along a hot and dusty road between Jerusalem and Emmaus after they had witnessed Christ's crucifixion. Even as they wondered why God hadn't shown up, Jesus came and walked alongside them (Luke 24:13-27).

What is surprising—and encouraging—about such encounters is that they are so ordinary. If you were to make up a story about meeting Jesus in the flesh, what would he look like? I would have him glowing like the sun, maybe with some levitation, lightning in his hands and thunder in his voice. There would definitely be lasers. But that's typically not how it happens.

In 1995, singer Joan Osborne asked a pretty perceptive question: "What if God was one of us? Just a slob like one of us? Just a stranger on the bus?"[2] In the case of the New Testament, he was like one of us. What makes us think it would be much different now?

In the plight of the homeless, the abused, and the

disenfranchised in the struggle against injustice or the difficulty of loving people who are just so frustratingly different from us, God is there. In the heartbreak of betrayal or the crucible of sickness, God is there. He inhabits the difficult places in our lives and in the lives of others, so we need not be afraid to go there.

Maybe you're still waiting for lasers and lightning. You're waiting for a clear, booming voice from heaven before you have the courage to follow Jesus into the prickly underbrush of your everyday life. What you may not realize is that you've already been given what you need in order to follow him with confidence.

Ask yourself, why did God bother to raise Jesus from the dead? Why not just take Jesus straight back to heaven and bypass the corporeal interlude? Instead, Jesus was raised in a physical body and appeared to hundreds of people over the course of forty days. Why?

Because his death and resurrection were not just so you and I can go to heaven one day and in the meantime idle our lives away with halfhearted morality and unsingable hymns or feel-good praise choruses. It was not so we can get "churched-up" on Sundays and live in blind indifference or passive apathy on the days in between. The visitation of the resurrected Jesus was meant to signal to us that a new reality has been unleashed in the world. That the presence and power of Jesus are here *now*, and they are healing and restoring amid the barbs and briars that we call life. Christ's resurrection shows us that his life, hope, healing, and renewal are happening today, in this place, in our world.

Sociologist James Davison Hunter says it well,

> The Son of God . . . was both the actual presence and
> the harbinger of a new kingdom. Everything about
> his life, his teaching, and his death was a demonstra-
> tion of a different kind of power—not just in relation
> to the spiritual realm . . . but in the ordinary social
> dynamics of everyday life. It operated in complete
> obedience to God the Father, it repudiated the sym-
> bolic trappings of elitism, it manifested compassion
> concretely out of calling and vocation, and it served
> the good of all and not just the good of the commu-
> nity of faith. In short, in contrast to the kingdoms of
> this world, his kingdom manifests the power to bless,
> unburden, serve, heal, mend, restore, and liberate.[3]

In other words, the resurrection of Jesus says, "Don't wait for
heaven. I want you to experience and participate in my healing
presence now. I am here, in this world and for this world. I am
in the briarpatch. Won't you join me?" If Jesus came to heal
the world, it makes sense that we would find him amid the
bristles and barbs where people are scratched up and bleeding,
where healing is most needed. If we want the fullness of Jesus'
resurrection presence in our lives, we cannot be afraid to admit
that we struggle and get lost in the tangle of suffering, doubt,
and discouragement. Yet we cannot be afraid to step into the
thorny thickets of our world because that is where the Savior
of the world does some of his best work. And he invites us to
join him.

CHAPTER 2

WE'RE NOT IN KANSAS ANYMORE
CLEARING THE LAND MINES

Home is not where you live,
but where they understand you.
CHRISTIAN MORGENSTERN

In the time of chimpanzees,
I was a monkey.
BECK, "LOSER"

It was one of those idyllic October afternoons in Atlanta and I couldn't take my eyes off the tattoos. From my home in the eastern suburbs, I had come into the city to meet Howard, a friend from the southern suburbs, for lunch. If you know anything about the sprawl of Atlanta, it will not surprise you that this meant we lived more than an hour and a half from each other, so we decided to meet in the geographic middle, about four miles east of Midtown, in the historic and artistic community of Decatur, which is tucked snugly against the inner edges of Atlanta's city center.

We found a restaurant on the quaint city square and settled at a table on the sidewalk. I had no idea that I would come to know this area well through the years, even becoming a regular, and it would be in this very community that I would learn to follow Jesus into places I didn't know existed. But on this day, it was a foreign land full of strange people, and I found myself thinking, "We're not in Kansas anymore."

At the table directly across from me, a lesbian couple sat with their young daughter. I had heard of such people before and had even seen them in the movies, or protesting one cause or another on the evening news, or yelling at the narrow-minded pundits on the political talk shows, but here they were . . . eating! And they weren't angry. In fact they were exceptionally polite to their server and sweet with their daughter. They were actually nice and happy. Who knew?

On my right was another challenge to my paradigm of propriety: two men, early thirties, covered in tattoos. *No doubt hardened criminals*, I thought to myself, *recently paroled after serving time for attempted murder, domestic assault, or sticking up a convenience store.* Were they casing the place, planning to return at closing time to clear out the register or maybe even the safe? They probably got those tattoos in the joint—the same place they learned to sharpen a spoon into a shank or trade cigarettes for a cell phone. But here they sat, these obvious felons on parole, drinking beer and smoking cigarettes, unaware that I had already planned my escape route in the event one of them should suddenly snap.

Glancing back at the table behind me, I saw a grandmother with her daughter and granddaughter, eating pita and hummus and sipping sweet tea, utterly oblivious to the mortal danger lurking just two tables away.

Just then, a group of men in very expensive suits sat down about ten yards down the sidewalk. When I had been looking for parking, I had noticed the county courthouse was just across the square, so I surmised them to be lawyers. They looked well-groomed and self-assured. Maybe at least one was an assistant district attorney. If so, he was probably packing a sidearm and knew how to use it. Yet none of the men seemed to notice the inked-up duo. Surely they had played a part in putting them away at some point. I finally concluded they must just be playing it cool and had things under control, so I could relax and enjoy my lunch with Howard.

Howard and I are both pastors, and he and I have been friends since our days in seminary. He was going through a rough time in his church, so we talked a lot about that. I was in the process of figuring out where I wanted to plant a church. We talked about that as well.

I had searched all over the country for a place to start a new church and had thus far come up empty. I knew I wanted to escape the suburbs—not because they aren't a great place to live and full of wonderful people, not to mention the neighborhood swim and tennis clubs and sprawling, manicured lawns, but because I had a sense, a growing and palpable yearning really, that God was calling us to go to a place different from any we had lived before. He was calling us out of our safe haven to love and serve people with whom we thought we had nothing in common. The only question for me was, *Where can I find a place like that? What will that even look like? Will I know it when I see it?*

MAKING A HOME

As we approached the end of our lunch, I remember asking Howard, "Where do you think all these people would go to church?"

"Not my church."

"Yeah, mine neither."

Pretty much every church I had ever been a part of had been the same—white, upper middle class, Republican capitalists (or at least young people aspiring to that). Everyone was just like me. Even Howard, who is black, would not be comfortable in the homogenized and pasteurized churches I had served thus far, though we're part of the same denomination. I'm not being critical. They are great churches, as long as your skin is a blank white canvas, your belief in God stable, your voting record socially and fiscally conservative, and your attraction fixed firmly on the opposite sex.

"What would a church have to look like for all these people to feel welcome?" I mused.

Howard didn't have the answer, and neither did I. But it was a question that would hound me day and night.

In the weeks that followed, my wife, Carrie, and I went on several dates in Decatur. We began to fall in love with the music and arts, the restaurants and pubs, and even the weird, eclectic mass of humanity. Amazingly, we began to realize we had found our home. This is where we would start a church and raise our family, but we knew there was a lot of work to be done—mostly in us. In Decatur, we would need to identify and defuse many cultural and ecclesiastical land mines. Much of how we understood—and were accustomed to communicating—the gospel would be lost in translation in a place like this. It would be the height of arrogance to presume to communicate the message of Jesus to a people I refused to try to understand; and I could not pretend to understand them unless I learned to truly love and appreciate them in all their beauty and wonder. But that would mean learning to see them as human beings created in the image of God, with dignity and worth. That's not so easy to do when you're not used to being around people with the name of an ex-girlfriend tattooed on their neck, or two women holding hands in public, in front of God and country. For me to see them through the eyes of Jesus, I would first need to deal with my own fears, elitism, and self-righteousness. Those are land mines that are hard to find, much less defuse, in our own lives.

THE MORE THINGS CHANGE, THE MORE THEY STAY THE SAME

For the past several decades in particular, the church in America has been fighting a "culture war." If you're not a Christian, don't watch religious broadcasting, or don't listen to conservative radio, you might be blissfully unaware of the battle being waged for the soul of our country. Assaults have been launched against network programming, children's entertainment and toys, and theme parks. Christians have been encouraged to retreat from involvement in the secular entertainment culture and instead find their orbit in a parallel universe of sanctified music, movies, books, fashion, and even breath mints. More than thirty years of these skirmishes have produced little more

than bitterness, cynicism, and incredulity on the part of many
people outside the church, and as I look at the shrapnel littering the cultural landscape, I have to say that, in many ways,
their cynicism toward the Christian establishment is justified.
Out of a sense of self-protection, not wanting to be compro-
mised and corrupted by the surrounding culture, Christians
have built an immense gulf between their own lives and the
lives of everyone else. This has created an emotional and relational disconnect that can make it quite difficult to navigate
the ground that regrettably separates life in the pews from
everyday life with the people and places we love and enjoy.
Before we can get to a place where serious spiritual conversations can take place, we must realize that the cultural ground
has shifted beneath our feet. The church no longer finds itself
in the 1950s, sharing the same mores and values, by and large,
of an American civil religion. The terrain is moving, and
though our foundation in the gospel of Jesus Christ remains
firm and certain, our steeples are cracking.

Timothy Keller, pastor of Redeemer Presbyterian Church
in New York City, describes this phenomenon well:

> Our typical evangelistic presentations are effective
> with persons who assume they should be good.
> Then the gospel-presenter tries to show them that
> they are not good enough—they fall short of God's
> perfect standards—and therefore they need Jesus
> to forgive sin and help them do the right thing.
> This presentation was quite appropriate for almost
> everyone in my parents' generation. My parents, who

are evangelical Christians, and my in-laws, who are
not at all, had basically the same social and moral
values. If you asked them questions such as, "What
do you think about premarital sex, or homosexuality,
or pornography?" both sets of parents would have
answered the same. They were part of a world in
which Christianity was the folk-religion even if it
was not the heart-religion of most people. They
believed that the purpose of life was to be a good
person. This world no longer exists everywhere.

On the other hand, if you say to those in my kids'
generation, "You know you have to be good," they
will say, "Who's to say what good is?" So what are
we to do with these post-everything persons who are
increasingly dominating our society? The traditional
gospel presentations will not make much sense to
many of them.[1]

In other words, we can no longer rely on a shared, trans-
cultural view of right and wrong, much less assume an innate
desire to know and follow God. Gone is the modernist's
confidence in rational persuasion or appeals to the innate
goodness, integrity, and rationality of humanity. The last vestiges of that worldview went out the window with Rwanda,
Darfur, and the collapse of the towers in New York. And
the killing of Osama bin Laden has done nothing to bring
it back.

So, whatever "postmodernism" is—and I'm not sure
anyone really understands what it is—it is different from

modernism. Things have changed. There are no longer universally accepted "spiritual laws." Appeals to innate morality don't so much fall on deaf ears as they are completely lost in translation. But this does not mean that Christianity has no appeal, that there are no bridges to be constructed across the crevasses created by the shifting landscape of our culture. We can build these bridges based on the *experience* of love, hope, and true transformation that we live out in our neighborhoods and workplaces because we have been changed and shaped by Jesus Christ. The world may be shifting, but our foundation remains solid and secure.

The timeless and true gospel is still the same story that transcends the ebb and flow of human history and remains relevant for our lives today. Our world has changed, but it is still the world that God loves and is redeeming. People have changed, but they are still people and they still need Jesus. Our job is to meet them where they are, not where we want them to be, even if where they are is prickly, uncomfortable, and not very tidy. After all, that's where Jesus meets *us*.

The message of the life, death, and resurrection of Jesus still speaks honestly to real hurts and doubts, to the real concerns and joys that we—and our neighbors—experience every day.

So where do we begin?

CONNECTION BEFORE COMMITMENT

When Brian first joined our worship band, he was well-entrenched in his skepticism of religion, but he needed the money.

Life for most working musicians is a far cry from the glamour and luxury we imagine—long days on the road, traveling from one small town to another, playing until a few hours before dawn, and then back in the car to drive to the next town. The couple hundred dollars per show barely covers the rent, so for Brian, finding a semi-regular paying gig at a church was a miracle of good fortune. He decided he could tolerate being in such close proximity to religious zealots who were out of touch with the way real people think and live if it meant being able to pay his bills.

Right from the start, it was a happy, symbiotic relationship. We needed him just as much as he needed us.

For the first year or so, Brian showed up on the Sundays when he was scheduled to play and became a delightful part of our mostly volunteer team of musicians. During the sermon and Eucharist, he busied himself in the lobby, loading up on caffeine and biding his time until he had to play the next song. He wasn't being paid to listen to the preacher and was more than happy to opt out, thank you very much. But he really liked the other musicians. They weren't so bad—talented, creative, sarcastic, funny. You know, real. They had become friends, but the religious stuff just wasn't for him.

Then I noticed he began to stay and listen to the sermon, tucked away in the back so he could slip out when Communion started. I kept my observation to myself and watched his friendships expand beyond the teams of musicians.

A few months later, Brian showed up on a Sunday morning when he was not scheduled to play. I was intrigued, but

I didn't ask him about it. I just said hello as he was talking to a group of friends after church.

A couple of weeks later, he stopped me in the lobby after the service.

"Can we talk?"

"Sure. What's up?"

He didn't seem nervous or fidgety. Rather, he had the knowing posture of someone who was about to ask a question that he already knew the answer to, or who had found something he didn't know he was looking for.

"I wasn't raised in church and have always believed that God was the stuff of fairy tales," he confessed, "but there is something different about you people. God seems real here. I mean, nobody tries to pretend they are perfect or always right. Nobody has all the answers, and you really seem to like each other. I have never seen a group of people who are so different from one another actually love each other like this."

He surmised, rightly, that there was a God thing happening.

We talked about Jesus, but Brian already knew him better than he realized. He had encountered the reality of Jesus in our community of faith, and it was an experience that was more real, and more convincing, than the most expert arguments from the best theologians.

"Initially," he admitted, "I decided to sit through the sermons so I could dismantle your arguments. I was convinced that Christianity couldn't stand up to rigorous intellectual scrutiny. After a while, I found myself swept into the story. You answered some of my questions, but always left me with more things to consider. Eventually, the reality of Jesus began to outweigh my objections."

As I watched Brian find his place in our midst, I realized something interesting: No one had tried to "witness" to him in any formalized, programmatic way. We had made room for him—not just in the pew, but in our lives. He had observed that Jesus does more than just change our religious habits, he shapes the entire story of our lives, and that's what made the difference. Even more important, he identified with our community of faith *before* he identified with Jesus. Vital to our responsibility in helping people find their identity in Christ is to make room for them among us. This is not an easy thing to do and may require that we abandon many of our assumptions and change a great number of our habits. It means we will always have people in our churches and in our closest relationships who don't believe in God. They have questions—good questions, hard questions—that we cannot be afraid of, even if we can't always answer them. Our friends must feel the freedom to doubt and rant and come and go as they please as they work out their place in our communities of faith as ones who, likely, do not yet share the faith. The community is vital. Connection to a believing community most often happens *before* any understanding of the gospel or its implications for one's life—before any commitment to following Christ.

In our church, we celebrate Communion every week. It is the heart and center of our worship and the foundational expression of our identity as Christians. It is a sign and seal of *who* we are and *whose* we are, and it reminds us that we cannot separate our identity as Christians from our inclusion in the church—a *community* of faith. To be a follower of Jesus is, by definition, to be a part of his body (Romans 12:5). Our participation in Communion is a corporate and collective reminder that we have thrown in our lot with this diverse group of weak and strong, broken and healed, ordinary people who love Jesus yet struggle with the same hurts, doubts, and foolishness we all do. An invitation to Christ must not be divorced from an invitation to identify with a new community—this community. Communion is our weekly reminder that individual faith and identification with a community of faith—the often stumbling and stuttering people of God—are two sides of the same coin.[2] Conversion may be more than identification with the community of faith and its communal life, but it is not less.

This idea is not as strange and alien to your neighbors as you may think. We live in a culture that places high value on communal identity—neighborhood, office, sports teams, clubs, school. We all naturally define ourselves relationally, by our social structure, and part of the "conversion" process entails a change in our primary, defining communal identity. As we have said, people will most often identify with a Christian community *in some form* before identifying themselves personally as a Christian. Is your church a place where that can happen? This is why at our church we say, "All Souls is a place where you can belong before you believe."

This has *huge* implications for how we think about the life of the church. The customs, character, and unconscious habits of our church family become vital factors in communicating who belongs and who doesn't. Every church has a set of values, which often are not the ones so eloquently written in slogans and mission statements. Rather, they are communicated explicitly, and implicitly, in the habits and attitudes of the people who make up the community of faith. From the moment a person walks through the doors, the ethos is absorbed and interpreted—the polite avoidance of the interracial couple, awkward glances at the sleeves of tattoos, or visible judgment of the two women who clearly are not just roommates. Most of us would never dream of telling people they are not welcome in our church, but that is nonetheless the message we send. And it is received loud and clear.

We unwittingly step on cultural land mines by confusing faith with political ideology, or with what we deem to be socially acceptable appearance and behavior, and we don't seem to realize that our friends outside the church see our blunders and stay away for fear of becoming collateral damage. We also litter our own turf with land mines set to maim anything that lacks Christian propriety—whether in appearance, belief, or lifestyle—in an explosion of disapproval, judgment, and rejection. We have been unable, or unwilling, to intentionally clear a relational path through the cultural and religious minefields. Our friends who are curious but do not believe or behave as we do turn around and walk away before even having the chance to dare to believe that God could love them.

I am convinced that the reason most people avoid our communities of faith—where Jesus can be discovered and known—is not the preaching, music, liturgy, or lack of programs. It is because of our own corporate self-protection and judgmental attitudes toward anyone who does not look, act, or believe like us. We are unwilling to take the risk of following Jesus into the briarpatch of welcoming and embracing our friends who don't fit, for whatever reason, into the refined and genteel Christian subculture.

Instead of taking its rightful place as the primary expression of the grace and peace of God, the church has too often been relegated to a place of irrelevance in our society, seen more as an exclusive club for people who believe, behave, dress, talk, and vote alike. All others need not apply.

LEARNING THE LANGUAGE

In our faith communities, the language we use to communicate life with God will create either an open door or a barrier, but it will almost never be neutral. As I began to think about the dozens of friends in our congregation who do not consider themselves Christians in any sense of the word, I wondered how foreign and meaningless our Christian lingo must be to them. It's easy to forget that we use a highly specialized vocabulary that often doesn't translate beyond the realm of lifelong, scrubbed-behind-the-ears Christians. For the average person on the street, it is either misunderstood or altogether nonsensical.

God brought this issue to my attention through a young woman in our congregation from Sri Lanka. Along with 70 percent of her fellow countrymen, Dayani was raised as a Buddhist. Her father was a Buddhist monk before giving it up in order to marry. He is still an influential and well-respected member of his community, where Buddhism defines family, faith, and national identity.

Dayani was invited to our church by a neighbor and has been attending for about two years, literally every week. Demure and shy by nature, she sits quietly in the front row, soaking in all the strangeness of a Christian worship service, which is so foreign to anything she experienced back home. I always say hello when I see her, and wonder to myself what she thinks about all of this. As I've learned a little of her story, I can only imagine the religious and cultural vertigo she experiences on a weekly basis. Her English is excellent, but unencumbered understanding is not to be taken for granted. How weird this place must seem to her. Not only are we speaking in a tongue that is not her native language, but she never heard much about Jesus before now, and concepts such as grace and forgiveness are equally exotic to her.

Being perpetually in the front row, Dayani is always in my line of sight as I stand in front of our congregation. I began to notice that whenever I mentioned concepts such as *justification* or *atonement* or *repentance*, she would furrow her brow in confusion and jot down notes, presumably reminders to consult a dictionary later. The words and ideas that came so easy to me were a bizarre and perplexing barrier to her coming to terms with Jesus and what he means for her life. In my sermons, I tend to avoid the ten-dollar theological terms that nobody understands or cares about, and try to make the themes and truths of the Bible meaningful and accessible by avoiding inflated and weighty terminology. But now I realized even that was not enough. Dayani understood English well enough; the greater problem was all the Christian jargon that was rich in meaning for those already well-schooled in the Christian life, but was utter gobbledygook to her, and probably to many others as well.

We take language for granted, but it is essential to our understanding of our world, new ideas, and even meaning. As human beings, language is our essential medium of expression in society—more than art, music, or sex. Language can either be a hindrance or a help to understanding. The same holds true when one begins the process of entering into a community of faith. For someone who was not raised in the church, walking through our doors must feel like being dropped in the middle of a strange tribe. We're all speaking English, but the dialect doesn't make sense.

Put yourself in the shoes of a non-Christian, whether Buddhist or run-of-the-mill agnostic, walking into your church. When they hear words like *sin*, *faith*, and *redemption*, or phrases such as *answer to prayer* or *sacrifice of praise*, at best they will have a vague notion of what they *think* those words mean. More likely, they will have no idea what you're talking about. Either way, it will give them a sense that they don't belong—like there is a collective inside joke playing out and they are the only ones being left out. In secular conceptual language, there are no analogs for terms like *sin* or *sacrifice of praise* as they are used and understood in the church. Instead, we sound like aliens. It is not only confusing, but insulting and threatening as well.

So part and parcel of loving our secular culture and clearing the land mines is helping them to understand the meaning of the "Christian language." We must define our terms and allow people the opportunity to see what *praise* looks like, or what *repentance* looks like in the community of faith.

The German philosopher Ludwig Wittgenstein, in his discussion of the use of language, gives the example of a chair. "If there could be no visual picture of a chair," he writes, "the word would have a different meaning. That one can see a chair is essential to the meaning of the word."[3] We understand what a chair is by virtue of our experiences with chairs. A chair is something we sit on, reupholster, or stand on to change a lightbulb; it is something we trip over in the dark and on which we stub our toes. Without these experiences, the term *chair* would be an empty concept.

To be understood, ideas and concepts must be both explained and lived out. So instead of using the word *sin* and assuming everyone knows what we are talking about, we can say, "Sin is all those things we do that we know are wrong and try to keep secret, that mess up our lives and hurt others, and that keep us from living the life of joy and peace God desires for us." Even someone who has a relativistic view of right and wrong will understand that. Don't assume. Tell them what you mean.

But once we have explained these unfamiliar concepts, we must live them out as well. Non-Christians will come to understand what an *answer to prayer* is by participating in a community of faith in which *prayer* is carefully defined in terms that are understandable to outsiders, and in which prayers are boldly offered to God and answered. The same goes for words such as *redemption* and *repentance*. We must be careful to first define what they mean, use them in ways that make sense to non-Christians, and be willing to live them out publicly.

To reach our culture, we must understand that much of our vernacular is utterly foreign to outsiders, placing an unnecessary barrier—a land mine—in the way of their coming into a life of faith in Jesus. Take the word *God*, for example. We know that when we say *God*, we mean the Father of the Lord Jesus Christ, the sovereign Creator of all things, the lover of our souls, the Holy One. He is the one we worship and submit to, on whom we depend, and to whom we pray and confess. But what about a person who has never prayed, never confessed, never seen life as anything more than living for the moment? To that person, the term *God* is an empty concept. Yes, we even have to define what we mean by the word *God*!

A few months ago, I noticed that Dayani had begun to sing along to some of the songs and join in with the liturgy and prayers. A few weeks ago, she asked to speak with me and we made plans to meet the next morning.

In my office, she said, "At first, I did not know what you were talking about, but I could not stop listening. But then I understood." She began to recount how God had captured her heart and how she had fallen in love with Jesus, who she now understood had forgiven her and given her life new meaning. She now believes that Jesus is who he claims to be—Lord, Savior, God. She said she prayed to him a lot and felt that he was there with her, in her house and at her work.

"Is this normal?" she asked.

"Yes!" I assured her.

She continued to talk about the overwhelming sense of

love and acceptance she now had. Finally, she asked, "Pastor Shayne, how do I become a Christian?"

I smiled and said, "Dayani, I have some good news. You already *are* a Christian. Jesus has drawn near to you, and the moment you confessed with your mouth that he is Lord and believed in your heart that God raised him from the dead, you became a child of God." We then prayed and God's presence was palpable. The following week, Dayani was baptized.

WELCOME TO OZ

Prior to 1543, most of the world, including the church, held to the Ptolemaic model of the heavens, which means they believed the earth was the center of the universe. In that year, Copernicus published *On the Revolutions of the Heavenly Spheres*, in which he demonstrated that the motion of the heavens can be explained without the earth being the geometric center.

This was called the Copernican Revolution because it constituted a complete paradigm shift in humanity's understanding of the way the universe worked. The old system was overturned and replaced with a new one.

We need to remember that a life of following Jesus is nothing short of a revolution. It involves exchanging one set of beliefs for another, one way of understanding reality for another, one set of allegiances for another. It is an often terrifying and destabilizing shift that is not easy to navigate, so why make it even harder by using exotic language and keeping weird people at arm's length? Why do we unnecessarily demand that they change before being welcomed into our lives or into our churches? Why are we so afraid to simply love people the way they are, tell them about the affection that God has for them in Jesus, and welcome them into our imperfect lives?

Entering the briarpatch means nothing more than loving people where they are, clearing their path of unnecessary obstacles, and being willing to share life with them—and let the life of Jesus be evident in us. Our calling is to tell the story of Jesus in a language that makes sense, being sensitive to the fact that it will turn people's paradigms upside down. We have to patiently tell and retell the story, all the while warmly welcoming them into our communities of faith, even when they don't believe as we believe.

Our calling is to help people find themselves in the story of redemption and see the implications of the life, death, and resurrection of Jesus. And we must model for them what it looks like to follow Jesus in repentance and faith. Radical paradigm shifts are not likely to happen overnight. Rather, the experience is more like a web of reality and identity that often takes months or years to weave. We must provide the place, the language, the story, and the relationships that allow for this weaving to take place. We must be open, loving, and courageous. And above all, we must be patient.

CHAPTER 3

THE WAY IN
NAVIGATING
THE THICKET

I fear that Christians who venture
to stand on earth on only one leg will
stand in heaven on only one leg too.
DIETRICH BONHOEFFER

I met Melinda the day Carrie and I moved to Decatur. The
rumor had begun to spread that a preacher was moving into
the neighborhood, and this caused much consternation for
those worried about their property values and the amiable
neighborhood vibe that had prevailed up to that point. The
concern was that a preacher and his family would disrupt
the eclectic equilibrium of the neighborhood by introducing dogmatism and intolerance into the harmonious, open-
minded, heterogeneous brew. Melinda's job, apparently, was
to scout us out and give a full report.

The neighborhood truly was a diverse habitat of artists,
executives, office workers, professors, and musicians. With
the exception of the Hare Krishnas down the street, who

obsessively kept to themselves, and Michael, who was ordained as an Episcopal priest but gave it up to become a cake decorator and now had no interest in church, we were the only house with even the slightest religious veneer—much less a life-defining faith.

It did not take me long to figure out that my acceptance among my new neighbors would depend on whether or not I was willing to appreciate this multiform blend.

SECONDARY SCOUT TEAM

I saw them through the dining room window. Three young women loitering at the end of our driveway, each with a beer in hand, nudging one another and nodding toward the house. I had assumed that Melinda's deft reconnaissance mission a few days earlier would have cleared up all suspicion about the Wheelers. No Rush Limbaugh on the radio, no framed prints of televangelists on the walls, no weird shrines with candles or stacks of evangelistic pamphlets on the coffee table. Perhaps this young trio had not gotten the report. How else to explain why they were staring at our house like it was haunted or had been the site of a recent smallpox outbreak.

Finally mustering their collective courage, the women ventured up the driveway and rang the bell. I waited a few seconds so as to not make it apparent that I had seen them coming. As I opened the door, I resisted the urge to imitate Lurch from the Addams Family: "You raaang?"

Instead, I smiled and simply said, "Hello."

They stood silent for a brief moment. I imagined they expected me to be wearing a clerical collar or have the pointed miter of a pontiff perched on my head. My threadbare T-shirt and unshaven face likely did not match their anticipation of what the creature of the cloth would look like.

"We're having a block party and really hope you and your family can come," said the shortest of the three. She handed me a flyer with all the information. I asked the traditional questions about what we could bring and how we could help. As we chatted, the women noticeably relaxed, each with one hand hidden behind her back.

"Thanks for the invitation; we're looking forward to the party," I said as they turned to leave. "Oh . . . and one more thing." I smiled. "Do you hide your beer from everyone, or just me?"

They laughed. "Well, we didn't know . . ."

I laughed too. "Don't worry. I get it. It's weird to have a pastor for a neighbor."

I closed the door, more aware than ever of the stereotypes and mistrust I would need to overcome. What had Carrie and I gotten ourselves into? It was as if we were some kind of extraterrestrials. At that point, I had no idea what the neighbors' suspicions were rooted in, and I was even less certain about how to begin addressing their concerns. All I knew was that their apprehension made me feel terribly lonely.

My neighbors were skeptical and afraid of letting me into their world. I guess it wasn't *me* as much as what I represented by virtue of my vocation. I might be a fine person, but my religious proclivities had to be checked at the door so as not to infect our tolerant and inclusive neighborhood. The irony seemed lost on everyone but me.

On the other hand, I completely understood.

Often, the Christianity represented on television and in other media is patently judgmental, arrogant, and divisive. The image that people have of Christians is mostly centered on what we are against—or at least what a particular preacher or pundit is against. People see self-appointed prophets and itinerant preachers on the campus quad berating and bludgeoning kids for the clothes they wear and the food they eat, and wrongly assume that they speak for even a minority of Christians. They see the small church in Kansas whose members travel the country to protest at military funerals and express "God's hate" for gays, Jews, the nation of India, Catholics, and whoever else does not fit their myopic view of the world. It only makes sense that many people would want to keep Christianity at arm's length when the vast majority of what they have seen from those who claim to represent God is saturated with criticism and vitriol.

It is more important than ever for those who seek to follow Jesus—and believe that his life, death, and resurrection matter—to clearly live out our convictions in a posture of grace and humility. Many are so befuddled and embarrassed by the "Christianity" represented by overzealous street preachers, lifeless congregations, and ecclesiastical infighting that they don't even know how to begin to contradict the prevailing message being put before the world. They are simply not equipped with a vernacular of faith that speaks effectively to their friends and neighbors. The teaching in many churches often lacks a relevant and optimistic view of the gospel and the promise of Jesus to bring hope, healing, and reconciliation to the world. So when the topic of sharing their faith comes up, many Christians cringe, shake their heads, mutter to themselves, and typically say nothing.

Many Christians seem to feel as if they have to choose between two options: either keep their relational distance from neighbors and coworkers—maintaining superficial and safe friendships—or downplay their faith, and maybe even hide it. Sure, they're polite, they work on projects together, say hello at Little League games, and wave while out watering the lawn, but actually talking about their relationship with Jesus seems out of the question because there are just too many negative perceptions to deal with. And they would never dream of inviting anyone to church. They never express any view or opinion that might betray their convictions.

But there is another way. It is a way of both integrity and openness.

HOW RELATIONSHIPS WORK

Since the day of Melinda's initial fact-finding mission and intelligence gathering, she and I had had many conversations and had helped each other with a number of projects. Melinda and her partner, Karen, have no children of their own, but they really like kids, and Melinda is especially funny and adept at engaging with them. My young children adored them after several evenings of pizza and movies at their house. We were friends.

One day, I was helping Melinda and Karen move some bags of mulch for their garden. Our conversation went something like this:

"So you're pretty serious about this whole Christianity thing, right?" Melinda said as I grabbed another bag of mulch.

"I guess you could say that."

"But how can you identify with a group of people who hold up posters that say 'God hates fags' or say that Tinky Winky is damaging to children? I grew up Catholic and it just seemed as if they were against everything. I couldn't take it anymore."

Dropping the bag in place, I replied, "Well, those people on TV don't represent me and they don't represent Jesus. You can't assume they speak for anyone but themselves. In fact, I don't even *know* any Christians like that. By the same token, when I see a group of angry lesbians on the news wearing T-shirts with derogatory statements about men and screaming sarcastic chants in some parade or protest, I don't assume they represent you. When I see a rainbow bumper sticker that mocks Jesus, I assume it conveys the perspective of the person driving the car, not the entire gay and lesbian community.

"Being gay is a primary way you define who you are," I continued. "But just because you're gay doesn't mean you're anything like the minority of wackos in the gay and lesbian community. As much as I don't understand about your community, I realize it would be unfair to arbitrarily mix you in with the negative stereotype. As for me, I'm a Christian, and there are plenty of stereotypes out there about us. Some are deserved and some are not. But I'm not a stereotype any more than you are. We may not fully understand one another, but who says we have to? We don't have to fully understand or even agree with one another in order to love one another and be friends."

Melinda looked at me with a knowing grin and said, "Fair enough." We went back to making her garden the envy of the neighborhood.

There is so much misunderstanding between the church and the gay community—and most other people outside the Christian faith—because too few of us take the time to get to know one another and become friends. It is easier to stand on our convictions and pass judgment on anyone who doesn't believe like we believe or behave like we think they should behave. We assume our disagreement precludes us from loving one another, and that is simply not true. No relationship actually works that way. I have never had a friend or family member with whom I fully agreed. We differ, and differ strongly, on our convictions of faith, politics, social issues, music, the environment, and on and on.

Marriages don't even work this way, at least not the good ones. Every marriage is rife with misunderstanding, conflict, and seemingly irreconcilable opinions. G. K. Chesterton was right when he said, "Marriage is an adventure, like going to war." Granted, it is important that couples come to some sort of agreement on important issues like faith and raising children, but there will never be a shortage of things on which to disagree. Carrie and I have been married for twenty years and our well of conflict is far from empty. But the existence of conflict and disagreement does not relieve us of our responsibility to love one another deeply.

Think about your relationship with your parents. If you

are still communicating with them, there are certainly a number of things about which you disagree, perhaps strongly. But does that mean you don't love one another? Does that mean you refuse to celebrate Christmas with them or call them on their birthday? I hope not. I realize that parent-child relationships can be terribly complex and that abusive things can be said or done that necessitate a break in the relationship. But, barring abuse, we love one another through the disagreements and conflicts. It's the way human relationships work. I would even argue that such relationships are healthier than they would be without the conflict.

When you love a friend and disagree, you have three choices. You could *abandon* the friendship (and many people do), but that doesn't solve anything and it's not a sustainable way to live unless you plan to hole up in a cabin somewhere, far away from human contact, with only your thoughts—and maybe a cat—to keep you company. Another option is simply to *avoid* the topic of disagreement. Again, this doesn't help and only serves to build a veneer around your relationship. Or, finally, you could *address* the issue, talk about your disagreement, and seek to understand each other. Perhaps one or the other of you will be convinced to change your mind, but maybe not. Either way, you get to know each other more deeply, and if it is handled with grace and kindness, the trust between you grows.

It saddens me that Christians too often choose one of the first two options. Maybe you have a friend who initially had no faith convictions, but then converts to Buddhism. Gradually, you stop inviting him or her to join you for a movie or to go out to lunch, and the friendship withers and dies. Maybe that's what happened to you when you came to faith in Christ. It was almost as if some of your friends believed that Christians could not be interested in sports or art or music and the social invitations dried up. It hurts.

It is even more common for Christians to simply avoid the topic of religion with their friends. As a result, they end up hiding the most foundational part of themselves from people they profess to care for and love. That makes no sense. Could it be that faith is not the issue, but rather that one or both parties acts like a jerk when the subject comes up?

You can't truly love others without inviting them into the most treasured parts of your life. And you can't love them without being willing to enter into and seek to understand their lives, even when you disagree. Jesus doesn't command us to agree, but he does command us to love and serve and show compassion and kindness. But how do we do that when the issues are prickly? What does it look like for us to bring Christ into our relationships without being offensive or plastic?

Love.

Wow, that's deep. I sense the sarcasm; but hear me out. There's a reason John Lennon and Paul McCartney captured the world with their song "All You Need Is Love." They tapped into a longing and need that is deeply embedded in the human heart. It's there for a reason. It's the way in.

THE WAY OF LOVE

When I was growing up, my father was a sure and steady guide for me. In many ways he still is. He was a firm disciplinarian and had exacting standards, but he was also very affectionate. He taught me to honor my word, tell the truth, and show respect to others, especially to adults or those in positions of authority, and deviations from the standard were simply not tolerated. But he also hugged and kissed me, and told me he loved me every day.

Even then, I realized it was somewhat unusual for a kid to receive that level of consistent verbal and physical affection from his father, but I loved it. Even in front of my friends, I was never ashamed to receive such unabashed expressions of warmth and care. Some of my friends teased me, but most thought it was cool. The idea of an attentive, caring father was as natural to me as breathing. I knew what it meant to be loved.

I realize that many people were not as blessed as I was to grow up in such an emotionally supportive environment. Perhaps you are one who had to endure a childhood with parents who were emotionally absent, neglectful, abusive, or cruel. Maybe you never experienced unconditional acceptance and came into adulthood always feeling the need to prove yourself, believing that love and acceptance are much easier to lose than to find. We've all had relationships in which the other person's affection for us felt conditional and uncertain—like we had to earn it somehow; but when it comes from our parents, it tends to permeate our lives, becoming part of our emotional DNA. We carry that uncertainty into all our relationships, even our relationship with God.

Though my father was not a Christian, he prepared me

well to understand and accept the love of God. In college, when I was introduced to Jesus, it all made perfect sense to me. I knew I was far from perfect—and I have dozens of stories I could offer as proof—but because I knew my father loved me, I was able to grasp that God could love me too.

It all started when I met some Christians who just wanted to be my friends. We studied together, listened to music, talked about girls, and played basketball. They went to parties with me, but mostly to give me a safe ride home. They knew I wasn't a Christian, but they loved me anyway.

These friends often talked about Jesus like he was a real person who made a difference in their lives. Over time, I began to ask questions and they were always happy to answer. They told me how God's love for us—for me—was so great that he sent Jesus to die for our sin. I had always known there had to be a God, but he was typically packaged in judgment and wrath. *If God is out to get me,* I thought, *let him take his best shot.* In the meantime, I would go about my business.

But now I was hearing about God's love. God loved the world. God loved me. That was different and it made sense. That was the kind of God I could get behind. That was the kind of God I needed.

Love had paved the way to my finding life in God. The unconditional love of my father as I was growing up and the unconditional love of my college friends provided me with a path to the embrace of God that was clear and compelling. God and love—both giving and receiving love—just go together; one leads to the other. Look at how the apostle John puts it:

> Everyone who loves is born of God and experiences
> a relationship with God. The person who refuses
> to love doesn't know the first thing about God,
> because God *is* love—so you can't know him if you
> don't love. This is how God showed his love for us:
> God sent his only Son into the world so we might
> live through him. . . . If God loved us like this, we
> certainly ought to love each other. . . . If we love one
> another, God dwells deeply within us, and his love
> becomes complete in us—perfect love!
>
> 1 JOHN 4:7-12, MSG

It's like trying to find the beginning of a circle. If you love
others, you find God. You will know you found God because
you will love others. Which comes first, love or finding God?
I'm not sure it really matters.

The much more interesting question is, *why* do I love?
Before I knew Christ, I loved my family and friends because
they loved me. It was healthy and symbiotic, but it didn't
necessarily transcend the particular relationship. There was
no compulsion to love that came from outside of myself.
Now things are different. Deeper. There is a new center
and source for love. I love because God set the pattern for
love—grace, forgiveness, life, sacrifice, healing, reconciliation, and restoration—by sending his Son. They all connect,
like spokes on a wheel, to the hub of who God is and reach
out in his mission of love in the world. We have a blueprint
of God's generous love in the life, death, and resurrection of
Jesus. Still, *why* do I love? As a Christian, I love even those

who wrong me or don't reciprocate because I have experienced something of the transcendent love of God. How do I know that? Because I love more freely and broadly than I previously thought possible. And we're back in the which-came-first circle.

Sound confusing? I think it's supposed to sound that way. We are people who tend to like neat little boxes for everything. It helps us to make sense of the world—gives us a veiled sense of control. This is particularly true when it comes to our trust in God. We collect our five-dollar theological terms and arrange them into orderly categories, all in an effort to get a fuller picture of who God is, what he expects, what he likes and doesn't like, who he cares about and doesn't care about, what he will do and won't do, and so on. But then we read, "God *is* love." Huh? That's it? Of course, God cannot be defined by just one word, but I think John is saying that if you had to pick just one word, *love* is about as good a word as you will find. Start there.

That's a good reminder for all of us. Never stray too far from simple, unadorned, and unconditional love because in the mysterious ways of God, he gives life in and through love; he inhabits love. Thus, if we love one another, God's love becomes *complete* in us. Love paves the way for others to find God. It blazes a trail through the thicket and thorns of every life and every relationship and makes God real, tangible, knowable. And that's as true for you and me as it is for others.

We can all do this. And just because it's simple doesn't make it trite—or easy.

HEALING AND HARMONY

Laurel and I had been friends for just a few months when things began to fall apart in her life. She was pregnant with her second child when she discovered her husband had been having a long-standing affair. The tension mounted and came to a head shortly after their new baby was born. He was unwilling to stop seeing the other woman and moved out, leaving his wife alone with two very small children, a dog, and a broken heart.

I walked down the street and knocked on her door. I didn't have any answers, and I don't think she really wanted any at that point.

"I heard what happened," I said. "I'm really sorry."

She invited me in, and we sat and talked for a while. She cried understandable tears of hurt and anger. I offered no advice, but let her know that we, my family and I, were with her in any way she needed. She was not alone and didn't have to pretend to be strong. We would pray for her and believed that God would not abandon her.

There were many more conversations in the months to come. She and my wife became very good friends. Many nights, the three of us would sit on our back deck and talk under the stars. We would laugh and cry. There were flashes of anger and rumblings of hope. God was there and our love grew.

About a year later, tragic illness struck one of my children and Laurel had an opportunity to love us back. God was there, too, and love grew even more. Over the years, we have all grown in our relationship with God and have found him to be palpable and persistent among us. It all grew out of love.

Love taught us—as Lennon and McCartney wrote—how to play the game and how to be where we were meant to be. It was all we needed. Taking the time to love, truly love, paves the way to the life that is found in God. And that love-life of God flourishes when the thorns are at their thickest, if we have the courage to go into the briarpatch.

When we step out in faith and simply love the people around us, a wonderful harmonization begins to happen. We begin to sense that we *need* this, that it is a natural expression of our faith in Jesus. The two worlds of faith and friendship, of church and community, begin to sing together as one. A life-encompassing resonance emerges that, somewhere deep down, we had always known was there in faint whispers and echoes, but now the parts seem to play as one. All we need is love. It is the song God sings over us (Zephaniah 3:17) and desires to sing through us.

It is the sound of our lives in Christ blending with our lives in the world, and it is a melody we were always meant to sing. All you need is love, God's love.

We too often buy into the lie that our spiritual lives and the rest of our lives should be distinct and separate, with as little overlap as possible. We don't bring the world—our world of struggle and hurt—into the church, and we keep the church off the streets. That is, we fake it at church so as to not inconvenience anyone, and we keep our mouths shut in the world so as not to offend. But when we choose to compartmentalize our lives, we rob both the church and the world of life and vitality. The church is *full* of broken people in need of love, compassion, and understanding; and our neighborhoods, workplaces, and public venues are *dying* to hear the good news of the love of God. The realm of Jesus *is* the realm of the world, and the realm of the world *is* the realm of Jesus. To artificially separate the two makes no sense whatsoever. As children of God, we are built to sing the melody of his love in Christ in *every* area of our lives.

Dietrich Bonhoeffer describes the error of separating our spiritual and physical (relational) lives:

> As long as Christ and the world are conceived as two realms . . . bumping against and repelling each other, we are left with only the following options . . . wanting Christ without the world or the world without Christ—and in both cases we deceive ourselves. . . . There are not two realities, but *only one reality*, and that is God's reality revealed in Christ in the reality of the world. . . . The reality of Christ embraces the reality of the world in itself. . . . The theme of two realms, which has dominated the history of the church again and again, is foreign to the New Testament.[1]

In the Gospel of John, we read what is known as Jesus' high priestly prayer, in which he prays to God the Father concerning us, his people. He says, "My prayer is not that you take them out of the world but that you protect them. . . . As you sent me into the world, I have sent them into the world."[2] The purposes of God and the prayers of Jesus drip with compassion for the world—your world, my world, the one we traffic in every day.

Because our physical world is one of confusion and corruption, our presence as Christians is all the more critical—not because we have some magic elixir, but because we have the life of Jesus: compassion, forgiveness, hope, and healing. Jesus says to us in the Gospel of Matthew:

> You're here to be light, bringing out the God-colors
> in the world. God is not a secret to be kept. We're
> going public with this, as public as a city on a hill. If
> I make you light-bearers, you don't think I'm going
> to hide you under a bucket, do you? I'm putting
> you on a light stand. Now that I've put you there
> on a hilltop, on a light stand—shine! Keep open
> house; be generous with your lives. By opening up to
> others, you'll prompt people to open up with God,
> this generous Father in heaven.
> MATTHEW 5:14-16, MSG

To live as Jesus has called us to live takes a little courage and a lot of integrity. It means we have to stop pretending. You have to be *you*, and I have to be *me*—the real me—a person who is a strange mixture of faith and failure, belief and reticence, sympathy and stupidity. We have to live with integrity in the sanctuary and on the street. But we face a great temptation to mold ourselves into something, or someone, more palatable. If we hide our deep faith and our even deeper struggles, we fail to fully live out the grace of Jesus among the thorns.

In hiding, we create personas that are typically one of two types. Not wanting to come off as too "religious," we downplay our faith and the presence of Jesus in our lives. We hide our God-colors under a bucket. We shrink back from introducing God into a conversation about suffering or family or injustice or addiction. We hide God from our friends and neighbors, and in so doing we hide a significant part of ourselves from them too. Or as the second type, we go into religious hyperdrive and hover so far above the spiritual heads of our friends at church, at work, or at home, that we appear to be immune to the struggle, pain, and failure that is common to human life. We put on an *über*spiritual veneer that makes others feel like spiritual pygmies and makes Jesus seem like the stuff of spiritual fantasy.

What we need—what our neighbors need, what I need—is the freedom to live honestly and openly, to learn to apply the grace of the gospel in real life where marriages struggle, kids get sick, we hate our jobs, our anger management plans get derailed, and sometimes we maybe even drink a little bit too much, but where Jesus really is in the business of transforming the real world—our world—with all its thorns and thistles.

This is the path Jesus has called us to. It is a path of courage and compassion, resolution and healing that goes into the dark and difficult places of the world and brings the redemptive, restorative light of Jesus Christ. In the coming pages, we will follow Jesus along this path into the briarpatch—the places of suffering and struggle in our world—to find the hope and healing that his life, death, and resurrection bring. But before we look outward into the world, we must follow the path through our own frail hearts of fear and doubt.

THE

BRIARPATCH

WITHIN

CHAPTER 4

THE ICEBERG LURKS
DANGER BENEATH THE SURFACE

We would rather be ruined than changed,
We would rather die in our dread
Than climb the cross of the moment
And let our illusions die.

W. H. AUDEN, "THE AGE OF ANXIETY"

I remember learning in school about icebergs, the massive floating islands of ice that lurk in the frigid waters of the northern- and southernmost reaches of the world's oceans. The danger of icebergs, of course, became part of modern Western lore with the tragedy of the *Titanic* on April 15, 1912.

What we learned about icebergs is that only about 10 percent of the total mass of these enormous floating bodies of ice is visible above water. The greater part, and greatest danger, lurks silently beneath the surface. We now know that what we see on the surface indicates a much larger and potentially destructive bulk underneath. And so it is with our hearts.

We think it's enough just to deal with the 10 percent of

our failures and foolishness that everyone can see. We're too easily satisfied with changing our outward behavior, and we develop sophisticated filters that disguise the destructive sources of arrogance, selfishness, and pride in our lives. We live the charade of politeness and propriety, diligently masking the frozen and potentially lethal ugliness underneath.

But an iceberg is still there, lurking, in all of us.

The Poisonwood Bible, a novel by Barbara Kingsolver, tells the story of missionary Nathan Price, who, in 1959, over his wife's reservations and objections, moves their family of four daughters from Georgia to the city of Kilanga in the Belgian Congo to convert that heathen African nation. Nathan is a machine, on autopilot for God. His zeal to "win souls" and do God's work is so consuming that he becomes myopic in his focus and blind to his own self-righteous arrogance, abusive posture, and cultural insensitivity. Completely wrapped up in his own world of prayer, Bible reading, and preaching—all things any good missionary should do—Nathan is completely unaware of the destruction he leaves in his self-centered wake. His family begins to resent him and the Congolese people do not trust him because he is inflexible and seemingly incapable of self-reflection. His obstinacy is a cover for the fear and insecurity that lurks just beneath the surface of his life, distorting everything it touches.

Lingala, the regional language used in Kilanga, has its own linguistic personality. Most words have wildly divergent meanings, often distinguished only by subtle differences in intonation or inflection. Nathan's wife and children become students of the language and notice these important distinctions. But Nathan, with his singular focus on "saving" the people of Kilanga through his preaching, teaching, and leadership, never catches on. He proclaims in his sermons each week that Jesus is "glorious" or "precious," but with his thick American accent and neglect of precise intonation, what the people hear him say is, "Jesus is a poisonwood tree." That is, Jesus is deadly.

Nathan's story becomes a comic tragedy as he loses the trust of the Congolese by his clumsy words, and alienates his family by his arrogant indifference to their opinions and needs. When one of his children gets sick and dies, he lathers on the religious platitudes and crushes his suffering wife with his unwillingness to comfort and his inability to mourn.

If we're honest, we can probably relate—more than we might like to admit—to Nathan Price's failure to peel back the surface of his foolishness and take a deeper look at what lies hidden underneath. It is sometimes too painful to deal honestly with the wounded and jaded parts of our being, out of which spring arrogance, folly, and insecurity. We cover up our resentments, loneliness, and deceit because we don't want to do the hard work of navigating through the thorns and thistles that dominate our inner life.

Even when we have a vague sense that something is deeply wrong, we ignore it. It is simply easier to deal with what we can see on the surface than to dive into uncharted waters. We maintain the delusional masquerade of outward holiness and "having it all together," all the while wondering why we are plagued with dissatisfaction and insecurity. We wonder why friendship and intimacy are so difficult, or why our marriages are flat and lifeless. We assume it must be everyone else's fault, and we remain completely unaware of the thorns growing around our hearts, even as they begin to break through the surface and prick those closest to us.

THE PROBLEM IS WITHIN

Jesus says the problem is *within* us (Mark 7:21-23), deep beneath the surface, hidden from sight, and (we think) under control. But no one can completely keep the thorns of arrogance, fear, hurt, and pride from poking through. They always break the surface sooner or later, no matter how hard we try to disguise or conceal them. Even the Pharisees, the religious professionals of Jesus' day, were unable to hide their inner icebergs of corruption from the eyes of Jesus—despite all their religious pretensions and their efforts to keep up good, spiritual, outward appearances. Jesus called them "whitewashed tombs" (Matthew 23:27)—a veneer of composure covering their decaying and dry-rotted souls.

Keeping up appearances doesn't deal with the real issues and never brings true change. The life of following Jesus means being willing to look beneath the surface. His presence brings renewal and restoration—not just to the world, but to our hearts as well. But the work of inner renewal is more demanding than we might think.

How do we know there's an iceberg underneath the whitewashed image we present to the world? Do you struggle with feeling inferior and have a controlling, consuming desire to make yourself look better in the eyes of others? Do you live with the constant fear of being unmasked as a fraud? Do you always have to be right, never able to admit when you have failed or been wrong? Are you afraid that if even your closest friends, or your spouse, knew what you really thought or what you really struggle with, they would stop loving you? Or are *you* unable to love, accept, and forgive others who fail you? If there's a disconnect between your inner and outer persona, there's an iceberg underneath. Guaranteed.

Allow me to give two examples.

In my work as a pastor, I see a significant amount of brokenness in people's lives. These problems do not discriminate on the basis of race, money, age, or gender. Everyone has problems. Some are worse than others, but no matter how much energy is expended to pretend and deflect, nobody is unaffected. Without question, the majority of problems are centered on two issues: money and sex. And not surprisingly, struggle in these areas is often just the "tip of the iceberg."

Let's first look at money. For most, the problem of money comes in the form of wanting it too much and obsessively trying to hold on to it. In other words: greed. An excessive desire for wealth and possessions is, quite simply, greed.

Well, he's not talking about me.

Am I?

Think about this: 85 percent of the world's wealth is held by only 10 percent of the people.[1] It is more jarring when you look at it the other way: 90 percent of the world's population lives on just 15 percent of the world's financial resources. If you own a home and a car and have even a meager savings account, you fall into the category of the world's financial elite.

Yet Americans—whether Christian or not—give away less than 2 percent of their income to charitable organizations or to the poor. Approximately 25 percent of Americans give away *nothing*.[2] Greed is not just rampant, it is *normative* and possibly the greatest threat to joy in our lives. Its tentacles are far-reaching, deep-seated, and deadly.

Jesus says, "Watch out! Be on your guard against all kinds of greed; life does not consist in an abundance of possessions" (Luke 12:15). Throughout the Gospels, Jesus tells us to "watch out" for fakes like false prophets and those among the Pharisees who insist on religious veneer over faith, and thus threaten the heart of God's life-changing purpose in our lives. The only other thing he gives such warning of is greed! Why? It's lethal.

In light of this, 1 Timothy 6:6-7 takes on a tone of compassion: "The joy of living as a child of God is the greatest riches anyone could have. You came into the world with nothing and you will leave the same way, no matter how much you acquire, so is it really that important?" (my paraphrase). At the very least, we should question the wisdom of giving our hearts to such things, deriving our identity or security from them. To do so makes no sense at all.

This is not to say it is wrong to have money, even a lot of it. But be aware of the trap. Whether you have a lot or a little, if your money is solely for your own pleasure and security, and you never think how you can do good with it, the roots of greed have already begun to grip your heart.

In the Bible, the warnings about greed are ten times more frequent than warnings about sexual sin. But people are put off by the church talking about money. "Why can't we focus on more important spiritual matters?" Based on how often it is discussed in the New Testament, there is no greater threat to our hearts than greed and money. There is nothing more likely to wreck our lives spiritually or scandalize the church collectively than our failure to look below the surface and our acceptance of greed as normative.

When we have a good year financially, get a promotion or a raise, or see an increase in our fiscal bottom line, we think, *Life is good.* We buy a new house or car, take a nicer vacation, and generally feel better about ourselves. Am I right?

When someone asks, "How's life?" is your answer affected by your portfolio or account balance? Are you even aware of how much the value of your home or the size of your salary affects your joy? But when we define life, even slightly, by abundance or lack thereof, our joy and contentment are in grave danger of being wrecked on the iceberg of greed as we drift away from the life God has designed for us to live. We *will* begin to lie, cheat, compromise, hoard, and ignore the poor in order to increase our vacuous contentment because we have become convinced that we cannot be truly happy unless we collect—and keep—more money. That is what it means for greed to be "a root of all kinds of evil" (1 Timothy 6:10). And that is why Jesus says, "Watch out!" The iceberg is lurking.

The problem with money is typically not how much or how little we have. Rather, the problem is that it becomes our identity. We rank ourselves against neighbors, friends, family, coworkers, and people at church based on whether we have more or less money than they do. Ask yourself how much your satisfaction with life is based on the number of digits in your savings account balance? How much of your optimism and hope for the future depend on the current performance of your stock portfolio (if you even have one)?

Getting below the surface is typically just a matter of asking a simple question: *Why is money so important to me?*

Only you can give the answer, but you must be brutally honest. Does it make you feel more important? Does it make you feel more secure? If so, why? If money is in the driver's seat, determining the level of your happiness and peace, what other thing or person have you relegated to riding shotgun? Something has been displaced, and it is probably God. When the money runs out, you lose your job, or the market crashes, who (or what) will be at the wheel? What, or whom, do you really want to be in control of your happiness and peace?

Now ask yourself the same question about sex. Why is it so important to you? Are you saying it's not?

In an average month, according to Safefamilies.org, 70 percent of men between the ages of eighteen and thirty-four visit a porn site.[3] In a poll of one thousand respondents, conducted by ChristiaNet.com, 50 percent of Christian men and 20 percent of Christian women were found to be addicted to pornography.[4] It is a multi*billion* dollar industry in which Christians actively participate. Though many pastors and ministries have been willing to take the bull by the horns to address this problem, the numbers suggest that the church at large doesn't want to talk about it.

Our society would say that pornography is no big deal.

Back in the days before the Internet, men collected stacks of magazines and proudly displayed them when their guy friends came over. No big deal. But how come when their wives, female coworkers, or moms stopped by, the magazines got shoved into a closet? Did they do the same with *Sports Illustrated* (other than maybe the swimsuit issue) or *Popular Mechanics*? I doubt it.

The use of Internet pornography in the workplace is epidemic.[5] Companies install sophisticated filters to keep their employees focused on work and off illicit sites. Let's say you're checking your flight status for your upcoming trip or reading the *New York Times* or even getting the score from last night's game. If someone unexpectedly comes into your office—or your wife walks into the room—do you rush to close the browser? No, probably not. What if it were a porn site? You would not be able to close that window fast enough.

We all instinctively know that pornography is wrong and destructive. And the vast majority of people who struggle with it feel terribly guilty about it. But ask yourself, "Why is living in a plastic, airbrushed, fantasy world of sex such a temptation for me? What void am I trying to fill?" To get at the answer, we have to look below the surface.

We are all built for intimacy, affection, and acceptance. Friendships, dating relationships, and especially marriage relationships are places where we get the relational care and closeness we long for. We want someone to know us deeply and accept us fully, even though nobody will ever do this perfectly. When it happens, it is truly extraordinary. We feel fulfilled and deeply satisfied, and it has nothing to do with sex.

But when we are lonely, bored, anxious, or feel rejected, we turn to a plastic placebo intimacy. It makes us feel alive, desirable, in control—for about ten seconds. But it is not true intimacy. It is an artificial adrenaline shot that hollows us out instead of filling us up. On the surface, it is "just some images," but underneath, it is tearing a lethal gash in the hull of your soul. Why do you think you need it? Go beneath the surface. Something is lurking underneath.

Here's some good news: When you follow Jesus, you have a safe environment in which to look beneath the surface of your life. You can be honest about your deeper struggles—and even run the risk of being rejected by people who will not be able to handle your weaknesses and failures. God sees everything—the 10 percent you show the world and the 90 percent of the iceberg below the surface—and he still loves and accepts you *completely*. What's more, the promise of Christ's resurrection is that your entire self *is being* and *will be* renewed as God puts this world to rights. Because the life, death, and resurrection of Christ are for *you*, you are actually free to be yourself—your true broken and beautiful self. You can come out of hiding. God is both your refuge and your strength (Psalm 46:1).

THE ROOT OF CHANGE

Pain in our lives often becomes the catalyst for us to go beneath the surface. Through suffering and adversity, we develop a hunger for change. We say, "I can't keep this up; something has to give. I cannot keep playing at church and religion. I cannot keep lying to myself or to my spouse."

Maybe as you're reading this your façade has begun to crumble. Maybe you're experiencing acute pain even now. You have no friends—true friends—because you keep people at arm's length for fear of being discovered. You are alienated from everyone who loves you because you are angry or bitter or have sacrificed relationships in your pursuit of success and significance. You live in constant fear of being exposed as hollow and shallow, and you wonder, *Can I change?*

Yes, you can, but it may mean you have to be brutally honest with yourself and with others, and risk being exposed as a fraud, a sinner, and a failure. But here's some more good news: The death and resurrection of Jesus was precisely for frauds, sinners, and failures like you and me. We simply need to apply the truth of Christ's resurrection to the deep places in our lives, the briarpatch in our hearts. You see, by rising from the dead, Jesus conquered the power of sin and death, setting us free to live our lives according to God's purpose for us. That's powerful!

GOING TO THE WELL

In John 4, we read about Jesus' famous encounter with the woman at the well. There was brokenness all over her life. The first was racial. When Jesus asked her for a drink, "the woman was surprised, for Jews refuse to have anything to do with Samaritans. She said to Jesus, 'You are a Jew, and I am a Samaritan woman. Why are you asking me for a drink?'" (John 4:9, NLT). The mutual disdain between Samaritans and Jews had roots going back more than seven hundred years (talk about deep-seated!) to a time when the northern kingdom of Israel, whose capital city was Samaria, was conquered by the Assyrians. After the conquest, some of the Israelites intermarried with the Assyrians, and their descendants, known as Samaritans, commingled the worship of God with Assyrian paganism. The Jews resented this and came to despise the Samaritans. The Samaritans promptly returned the favor. With that kind of history, Jesus wasn't supposed to talk to the Samaritan woman. But he did anyway.

There was also interpersonal and perhaps moral brokenness in the woman's life. When Jesus said, "Go, call your husband and come back," she replied, "I have no husband."

"You are right," Jesus said. "The fact is, you have had five husbands, and the man you now have is not your husband" (John 4:16-18).

We don't know the exact circumstances in this woman's life—she may have had five husbands who died, or been five times divorced, or she may have been a prostitute—but any way you look at it there was tremendous brokenness and pain in her past. The fact that she was at the well alone, in the heat of the day, suggests she was an outcast in her town, and her relationships with men had clearly been disappointing, and perhaps even destructive. And yet, here is Jesus—a Jewish man—peering deeply into her shattered heart, not to condemn her, but to offer healing in the form of "living water" (John 4:10).

You can almost imagine the look on her face as it begins to dawn on her that Jesus is more than a teacher and more than a prophet. With a certain degree of haste, she leaves her jar and goes immediately back to town, to the very people she generally tried to avoid. "Come, see a man who told me everything I ever did," she says. "Could this be the Messiah?" (John 4:29).

I want you to notice something peculiar—and very important—here. This woman was an outcast in her community. She went to great lengths to avoid interaction with the people who had rejected and shunned her. When she came to the well the first time, she was alone. When she came back, she was not alone. In fact, the New Living Translation says, "The people came streaming from the village" to see Jesus (John 4:30). Where once there had been animosity and resentment, now there is unity, agreement, and spiritual fellowship. "Now we have heard for ourselves, and we know that this man really is the Savior of the world" (John 4:42).

This woman, who had become a pariah because of her failure to live up to pretty much every standard of her society, found grace and acceptance in Jesus. She found a new standard: "If anyone is in Christ, he is a new creation. The old has passed away; behold, the new has come" (2 Corinthians 5:17, ESV).

Because Jesus "was delivered over to death for our sins and was raised to life for our justification" (Romans 4:25), I can say with assurance that God is okay with me, and God is okay with you. That's the power of the Resurrection. The question is whether we will live in that power and in the promise of God's divine affection. Much of the 90 percent that we try to keep hidden is tied to the fact that we don't believe God is okay with us. We think we have to be better, or at least appear to be. God's favor is not enough for us; we need the approval of others (or maybe more money) to be happy.

The power of Christ's resurrection gives us the freedom to ask ourselves the deeper, harder questions: "Why do I lie? Why do I avoid certain people? Why do I get so ridiculously angry at the smallest things? Why do I find it so difficult to forgive those who have wronged me? Why do I think pornography will ever satisfy me? Why do I feel as if nobody likes me?"

Then ask, "Do I really believe God when he says I am his beloved child in Christ? Do I believe that Jesus peers deeply into the ugliness of my heart and still offers me the living waters of his grace?"

Friends, true change will only come if it is rooted in the life, death, and resurrection of Jesus. Trying to put new behavior on top of flawed views of God and ourselves will only lead to frustration. Change must be rooted deep within our hearts, and our lives must be driven by the power of Christ's resurrection and the new standard of the gospel—that is, in Christ we are a new creation.

OUR STANDARD

Everyone has a standard by which they judge success and failure in life. This standard may be a loose identification with some sort of religion or moral code—go to church, "do unto others," keep the Ten Commandments. Or it may be a general, even nebulous, philosophy of meaning and value: Be true to yourself and leave the world a better place than you found it. The point is, everyone has a basis on which they evaluate happiness, worth, and success. Whatever your criteria, your life will always be divided into two parts—success or failure. You either live up to your standard and succeed, or you don't and you fail.

The problem is that *nobody* lives up to even their own subjective standards. Let's say, for example, that the Golden Rule is your standard of morality and meaning: "Do unto others as you would have them do unto you." Do you want people to scream at you or lie to you? No, you don't. And yet you lose your temper with your kids or perhaps tell a lie to cover up a mistake. So by your own standard you have failed. You can't live up to even the most basic principle of human interaction. Nobody can.

When you fail—and we all fail—you "repent" and vow to do better. But does that change anything? Probably not. You and I both know that it's just a matter of time until you once again treat others in a way you would not want to be treated—you're rude to a cashier, or gossip about a coworker, or entertain inappropriate thoughts about someone who is not your spouse. The point is, your standard is something you can never keep perfectly and it unavoidably leads you right back down the road to failure. Thus, your repentance begins to feel futile because it merely starts the cycle all over again. Discouragement—even cynicism—is inevitable and will lead to apathy. "Why try when I'm only going to fail again?" Even repentance begins to feel like a farce.

We need a different standard. We need an objective basis on which to judge our lives, one that is honest about our successes *and* failures and yet leads to "repentance unto life" (Acts 11:18, KJV).

The life, death, and resurrection of Jesus is a standard—the only standard—that can foster life and produce lasting change. Because of what Jesus did, the standard of God's law has been legally fulfilled for those who believe. Our repentance leads to life because, as Christians, when we fail to live up to God's standards, we repent *toward* the gospel—that is, we identify with the transforming power of the Resurrection. Our repentance is a repentance *unto life* because it drives us back to Jesus, the source and supply of our freedom. In our repentance, we admit that we cannot live according to our own standard; that we need another standard as our basis for acceptance with God.

We are led into success *through* failure. Becoming a Christian does not mean we no longer fail and our lives are now perfect. Neither does it mean we can live however we please because we know we will be forgiven. Rather, because our standard is now the life, death, and resurrection of Jesus, we become people who repent joyfully because our failure drives us back to our true standard of acceptance and hope (in Jesus). We are not afraid to go beneath the surface because the grace of Jesus goes there with us, reminding us that we—warts and all—are the beloved, accepted, cherished children of God. "See what great love the Father has lavished on us, that we should be called children of God! And that is what we are!" (1 John 3:1).

REMEMBER WHO YOU ARE

My first job as a teenager was working at the amusement park in our city. Though I was only fifteen, I was put in charge of running a booth that sold cigarettes and film. I had no means of processing credit cards, so all transactions were in cash. In the course of a day, I handled thousands of dollars. I had never seen so much money in my life.

The cash register I used was not computerized. It was one of those old analog types with buttons you had to mash and was not connected to a larger network. This was in the days when record keeping was still done with a pencil and a ledger sheet—not exactly state of the art. I assumed nobody would notice if I pocketed a little bit of cash for myself each day.

Over the course of a few weeks, I skimmed thousands of dollars from the till, yet I was convinced no one had noticed. Sure, I felt guilty, but my shame was assuaged by the roll of bills in my pocket at the end of each workday. I was getting away with it. Or so I thought.

I was right about one thing: The park's accounting method was full of holes. They would not be able to track a specific amount of missing money back to me. But I was wrong in thinking nobody would notice.

What I hadn't seen was the video surveillance camera set up across from where I worked that recorded me as I slipped bills into my pocket without ringing up the transaction.

It all came crashing down one day when the park's barrel-chested head of security, complete with handcuffs and surly demeanor, walked up to my booth with my boss.

"Mr. Wheeler, please come with me."

I almost threw up on the spot.

In his office, the security officer informed me that they knew I had been stealing money and asked if I wanted to see the tapes. Because they could not prove the amount I had stolen, they were going to fire me without prosecution. I was only mildly relieved.

I had to call my father to have him come pick me up four hours early. Of course, he wanted to know why. I told him.

Silence.

"I'll be right there."

Click.

I was devastated and convinced my life was over. My father had extremely high expectations of me, and I knew this was going to be a bad situation.

When he pulled up out front, I got in the car and immediately started crying. He didn't say a word.

After a while he said, "Son, this is not who you are."

He left it at that, allowing his words to sink deep into my soul. My father has always been known for his epic lectures. I would often wish he would just beat me with a stick or ground me for a year rather than continue with his rants. But this time his lecture was just six words long: "This is not who you are."

I knew exactly what he meant. I was his son. I had disappointed and failed him, but I was still his son and he still loved me. My failure and shame reminded me of who I was, and it actually strengthened and solidified my standing as a son. That's what grace does. Without minimizing our foolishness or sweeping it under the rug, it drives us back to our true standard.

When we fail, our standard will bring us either life or death. If our standard is the resurrection of Jesus, we are children of the living God and our failure, foolishness, and brokenness will drive us back into the embrace and acceptance of our Father. Your struggle with pornography, greed, or lying will cause you to be reminded of *who* you are and *whose* you are—just as I was reminded in the car that day. Galatians 2:20 says, "I have been crucified with Christ and I no longer live, but Christ lives in me. The life I now live in the body, I live by faith in the Son of God, who loved me and gave himself for me."

Friends, we need not be afraid of going deeper into the briarpatch of frailty and sinful idiocy that characterizes our hearts. To avoid the briarpatch is to avoid the grace that is ours in Jesus Christ and to miss the opportunity to be reminded of who we are. So go there. Ask the hard questions. Go deep. Jesus is waiting.

CHAPTER 5

VERTIGO
THE DANCE OF
DOUBT AND FAITH

I am plagued by doubts. What if
everything is an illusion and nothing
exists? In that case, I definitely
overpaid for my carpet.
WOODY ALLEN

Modest doubt is called
the beacon of the wise.
WILLIAM SHAKESPEARE

Have you ever had your life flash before your eyes? I have.

People usually say, "My life flashed before my eyes!" as
a way of communicating their reaction to a startling event
or a brush with death, but they often mean it only as an
idiom. Their life didn't *literally* flash before their eyes. But
mine did.

When I was twelve, some friends and I were hanging out
in the woods behind our apartment complex just outside
Nashville. There was a steep hill with a dry creek bed at
the bottom. It was full of massive rocks made smooth by
the spring waters that filled the creek each year. We used to
spend hours exploring up and down that creek, looking for

snakes and constructing forts. On this day, we were swinging on the long, woody vines that hung from the tops of the tall trees. We would get a running start and jump out over the bed of rocks, laughing half out of fear and half out of pure delight.

As the afternoon wore on, we began to hear cracking sounds in the vines as we swung. About the time we had decided to stop, for fear that one of the vines might break, a small group of girls came walking down the hill. At least one of them was really pretty and I was not going to miss the opportunity to impress her. I decided to take one more heroic turn. There was no way she would not be awed by my bravery and athletic prowess.

I grabbed the vine and walked up the hill—farther than before in order to get maximum speed and height. Steadying my nerves, I turned to the group of young girls.

"Watch this," I said.

Running full speed, I reached the precipice, where the slope became almost vertical, gritted my teeth, and pushed off with as much force as my little legs could muster.

Now I was sailing higher and farther than any of us ever had. It was epic. I would surely earn the adoration of the girls and the respect of my friends. I would be a hero, no . . . a legend.

Reaching the pendular crest, I felt that split-second sensation of zero gravity. Laid out almost vertically and hovering twenty feet above the rocks, my stomach dropped into my legs. I gripped the vine tighter.

At about the same moment, a loud, almost percussive,

crack split the air of the tiny valley. Instantly, I was falling, straight down, toward the rocks below.

That's when the movie started. Scenes from my life flashed before me: getting my first bike for my birthday; my sister teaching me how to read as we lay on the living room floor; chasing our new puppy around the tree in our front yard; looking out the window for Rudolph's red nose on Christmas Eve. One after the other they were seared into my mind's eye, until I struck a rock the size of a coffee table and heard the snap in my back.

The air rushed out of my lungs and I struggled to breathe. After what felt like an eternity, a man whom I had never met was standing over me asking if I was okay.

Eventually, I was able to breathe again, although not without a great deal of pain. As my friends rushed to get my father, the man helped me up the steep incline.

The doctor said I escaped paralysis by about half an inch. Had I landed just a little more to the right, my spine would likely have broken in two. Miraculously, even as I was so forcefully folded over a large boulder, I did not strike my head.

My body healed, but to this day I am terrified of heights. It's an irrational fear, I know, but I come by it honestly.

Of course, once you have a fear like that, it's amazing how often it is put to the test. There are houses to be painted, Christmas lights to be hung, trees to be pruned.

One Sunday morning a few years ago, I noticed a couple of burned-out bulbs in our sanctuary. The fixtures were about fifteen feet off the ground and our tallest ladder was a ten-footer, but I decided to brave it.

I stood on the next-to-top step with my shins wedged against the ladder's summit. ("This is not a step" written boldly before me.) I stretched up to reach the dead bulb, talking to myself like a lunatic in hopes of assuaging my fears. Legs shaking, sweat pouring, I discovered that if I looked straight ahead, the room would stop spinning and my body would become steadier. But as soon as I looked up to locate the bulb again, I was overcome by a sensation of falling. I knew I was relatively secure on the ladder, but some part of my brain was sending out vertigo-inducing signals. No matter how many times I muttered, "You're fine," as soon as I looked upward, I was convinced I was falling. Intellectually, I knew one thing to be true ("I'm fine"), but my brain and other senses seemed to have differences of opinion that completely threw me off balance.

That is often what faith feels like—an unstable, dizzying vertigo of the heart.

In our spiritual lives, we have times of intellectual clarity, even certainty, about the presence and affection of God. Yet our hearts are broken and confused by suffering—our own or others'—and the room begins to spin. We experience intimacy and peace with God even as our minds wrestle with theological, moral, or philosophical dilemmas to which we are unable to find answers. We know God loves us, but emotionally we can't believe he can forgive what we did. The result is doubt, a disconcerting (but ultimately healthy) companion to faith.

Often, doubt takes us by surprise. We are ashamed of it, even afraid, and don't know what to do. On the one hand, we don't want to turn our minds off and ignore the good and honest questions we have. That wouldn't be intellectually honest. On the other hand, we truly believe that God is real and good and loving, so cynicism and abdication of our faith are not an option, even though our uncertainty is often great.

What does it look like for us to doubt with spiritual and intellectual integrity? And why are we so afraid of it?

EVERYONE DOES IT

Doubt is a dirty little secret that many Christians, especially those of a more theologically conservative stripe, don't want to talk about. Even among friends, we feel the need to keep up an image of confident holiness, so we never give voice to the deep questions that plague our hearts and minds. So great is our fear of honest doubt that often we will not even admit our struggle to ourselves, much less to fellow believers. But you know, and I know, we all struggle with doubt—and that's perfectly normal.

Doubt is not veiled unbelief; it's merely an expression of uncertainty. It is seeing, hearing, experiencing, even knowing the reality of God and still asking, "How can this be?" It is the shadowy middle ground between belief and unbelief, and it is part and parcel of a rigorous and dynamic faith. In fact, doubt carries in it the seeds of faith. For example, in order to doubt that God is good or loving or just, we must first, on some level, believe that God is real and that he matters.

If you're a Christian and never have doubts or questions, you're not thinking seriously about your faith. C'mon, as Christians we believe that God became a man in the person of Jesus Christ. Is that even possible? Really? We believe that Jesus was crucified and then raised from the dead—not resuscitated, but *resurrected*. Really? Even the disciples balked at this initially. They lived and worked with Jesus during his earthly ministry, witnessed his miracles and his crucifixion; yet when the resurrected Christ stood before them, they questioned, "How can this be?"

And our doubts are not limited to the actions and claims of God. They often penetrate the realm of emotions and relationships. This sort of doubt is what Saint John of the Cross, the sixteenth-century Spanish poet and Carmelite priest, spoke of as the "dark night of the soul," in which we experience spiritual loneliness and desolation in our lives with God.

We mistakenly think that the spiritual giants among us live their lives with an unshakable spiritual confidence, or easily attain and maintain intimacy with God. That is most often not the case. In 1959, Mother Teresa wrote, "In my soul I feel just that terrible pain of loss—of God not wanting me—of God not being God—of God not really existing."[1] Her dark night stayed with her for more than fifty years. In one letter, she writes, "As for me, the silence and the emptiness is so great, that I look and do not see, listen and do not hear—the tongue moves [in prayer] but does not speak."[2] Yet Mother Teresa also knew of the deep and abiding joy of God—the "very special love" of Christ—that compelled her to serve among the world's poorest and most disenfranchised people in Calcutta and become known as "the Saint of the Gutters." Over time, she came to see that her own painful experiences of abandonment could help her identify more intimately not only with what Jesus experienced on the cross, but also with what the poor and marginalized faced on a daily basis. Mother Teresa's doubt was not so much contrary to her faith as it was a catalyst to it. Her roots grew deeper than most because they were forced to grow in the dry and rocky soil of suffering and doubt. Her honest struggle empowered her to embody the compassion of Christ in a way that few of us will ever know.

RUNNING THE RACE

A few years ago, I decided to train for and run a marathon. I've always been a decent runner, but in the beginning it would have been impossible to endure the rigors of a 26.2-mile run without building up my strength and endurance. Over the course of a year, I subjected my legs and lungs to longer and harder training runs, slowly pushing a little further and faster. My body became more proficient at processing oxygen, and the pounding of muscles, joints, and bones actually strengthened all three.

Endurance and skill increase only when you put in the miles. You will never develop as a runner without the challenge of training. So it is with faith. The testing that comes from navigating the briarpatch of doubts is a healthy and necessary element of a strong and enduring faith. Running the race of faith requires training. It is lazy, even irresponsible, to stuff our doubts and never deal with them honestly. When real intellectual and experiential challenges come up—and they will—we will find ourselves cramping and out of breath if we haven't built up our faith. Fyodor Dostoyevsky wrote in his personal notebook, "It is not as a boy that I believe in

Christ and confess Him, but my hosanna has passed through a great furnace of doubts."[3]

Timothy Keller suggests that doubt is a necessary part of our faith's "immune system":

> A faith without some doubts is like a human body without any antibodies in it. People who blithely go through life too busy or indifferent to ask hard questions about why they believe as they do will find themselves defenseless against either the experience of tragedy or the probing questions of a smart skeptic. A person's faith can collapse almost overnight if she has failed over the years to listen patiently to her own doubts, which should only be discarded after long reflection.[4]

We question the wisdom of parents who do not get their children immunized from potentially fatal diseases. We see it as irresponsible, if not neglectful or even abusive. And yet as pastors, Sunday school teachers, parents, and friends, we send not-so-subtle vibes of shame to those in our communities of faith who dare to question the actions, affection, claims, or even the existence of God. In so doing, we deny them the opportunity to develop the antibodies necessary for a deeper, healthier, and more mature faith.

THE TREADMILL

I met Dan when I was a youth pastor in Virginia. He was fresh out of high school and had recently become a Christian.

We got together regularly for coffee and talked about life. Over time, we became good friends.

Dan worked as a trainer at a gym, and though he was much smaller than I am, he was very strong and in excellent shape. For me, the neglect that went along with years of school and work and having a very young family had caused my body to bear some resemblance to Homer Simpson's—neither firm nor fit. I asked Dan for help and he invited me to the gym.

Our first step was to work on our "cardio," which meant running on a treadmill. I had been a runner in the past so I figured it would be easy. It wasn't. I huffed along at a snail's pace while Dan sprinted next to me with ease. He kept increasing his speed while I felt as if my lungs were about to explode.

The treadmills faced into the workout area, where several other people were going about their business. About fifteen minutes into our run, a fit and attractive young woman came into the room. I noticed her, but was far more concerned with the nausea welling up in my gut. I held on to the handrails for dear life as I tried to keep my legs moving with some semblance of rhythm. When Dan noticed the woman, he promptly increased his speed again, chest out, arms pumping.

As it happened, the woman walked directly in front of us, and as she passed, Dan's distraction reached critical mass. In a fraction of a second, and with a thunderous clatter, he lost his footing, did a face-plant on the belt, and was catapulted backward.

While I kept running and pretended not to know him, the entire gym stopped and stared as Dan lay on the ground, dazed and disoriented, unsure exactly what had happened and why.

This is what doubt often feels like. We're running along just fine but have drifted imperceptibly. Then we experience a thicket of reality that our hearts can't spiritually process, or we come across a thorny question we can't get our minds around, and it's like our foot hits the edge of the belt, or something else hangs us up, and down we go. In a heartbeat, our minds are clouded with doubt, we lose our footing, and we often don't even know why.

In Psalm 73:1-3, it seems that Asaph had a similar experience, as he described his struggle with doubt: "Surely God is good. . . . But as for me, my feet had almost slipped; I had nearly lost my foothold. For I envied the arrogant when I saw the prosperity of the wicked." Intellectually, he knew of God's goodness, but he became embittered by the inequity and injustice all around him. He was getting mixed signals, vertigo was setting in, and he almost lost his footing.

The injustice that Asaph wrestled with is a problem for everyone, whether we're followers of Jesus or not. You don't have to be a Christian to see that oppression and marginalization of the weak and vulnerable at the hands of the strong and powerful is wrong. And to be honest, Christians cannot adequately explain why God allows such injustice to happen. On the other hand, atheists have no response to injustice in the first place. If there is no moral God, then there is no place for moral obligation. If there is no God, then the strong crushing the weak is just the natural way of things.

In the face of injustice, suffering, inequality, and violence, is the only natural conclusion that there must not be a God? You might say that your outrage at evil is the reason you can't believe in God. But if there's no God, you have no basis for outrage because the God it is focused on doesn't exist. So you're back where you started. Outrage at injustice assumes there must be a basis for moral good; it assumes a good God. So injustice induces a vertigo of faith—also known as doubt—for *everyone*, even those who claim to have no faith.

A FOUNDATION FOR DEALING WITH DOUBT

It is a mistake to think that faith requires the removal of all doubt or that every question must be fully answered and every reality explained. There is a certain amount of mystery involved in life and love—things that just cannot be adequately articulated or explained. If you have ever been in love, you know what I'm talking about. Try explaining what it is to be in love. Even the best prose and poetry fail to plumb the depths, but does that mean that your being in love is any less real? No. In fact, it speaks to the very real extent to which it has gripped your heart.

Neither does it mean that love is not based in fact. The object of your affection is a living, breathing reality with physical, emotional, and relational attributes. True love requires a true object, which in turn requires empirical evidence. I love my wife because she is real—because I know what she says is true—even if she often remains an utter mystery to me.

It is the same with God. Even if we never quite solve the mystery of his being, there must be a basis of truth—objective, foundational evidence that he exists and that what he says is true. Nobody expects faith in God without evidence. Fortunately, we have plenty of it.

At the end of Luke 24, there is an extraordinary scene in which Jesus—the one who claimed to be God in the flesh— appears to his disciples after his resurrection. They are all gathered together, talking about the fact that Jesus has gotten himself killed and now they don't know what to do. As they converse, Jesus walks in—and they freak out, but not in a good way. They think they're seeing a ghost. I imagine them wide-eyed and knocking over chairs as they back away from this apparition.

Jesus says, "Why are you troubled, and why do doubts rise in your minds? Look at my hands and my feet. . . . Touch me and see; a ghost does not have flesh and bones, as you see I have" (Luke 24:38-39).

Jesus is saying, "This is not some stress-induced, meta-physical experience; I am physically, bodily here." He shows them the reality of his resurrection without explaining *how* it is possible. The disciples knew that dead people do not rise from the grave. The vertigo of faith swept over them and—it must be emphasized—they *had to be convinced*. What they experienced did not square with what they thought was possible.

As sophisticated, modern people, we're tempted to think that the disciples made up the resurrection of Jesus because they wanted it to be true. But in their Jewish paradigm, there was no belief whatsoever in bodily resurrection. Why would they make up a ludicrous story that they knew nobody would believe and that didn't square with anyone's concept of reality?

They wouldn't.

As Anglican bishop N. T. Wright and other New Testament scholars often point out, there was no room in the worldview of first-century Jews or Gentiles for immediate, bodily resurrection. They simply didn't believe that dead people could rise from the grave. The point I want to emphasize here is that the Resurrection surprised and shocked the disciples just as it would us. They didn't say, "Ah, Jesus, we've been waiting for you." Rather, they were deeply troubled. They doubted. And even after they saw clear physical, empirical evidence, "they still did not believe it" (Luke 24:41).

N. T. Wright says,

> It will not do, therefore, to say that Jesus' disciples were so stunned and shocked by his death . . . that they projected their shattered hopes onto the screen of fantasy and invented the idea of Jesus' resurrection as a way of coping with a cruelly broken dream. That has an initial apparent psychological plausibility, but it won't work as serious first-century history. . . . A Jewish revolutionary whose leader had been executed by the authorities . . . had two options: give up the revolution, or find another leader. . . . Claiming that the original leader was alive again was simply not an option. Unless, of course, he was.[5]

There were many messiah figures in the first century who died or were killed, yet there were never any claims made that they were raised from the dead. Why? Because everyone knew that dead people don't rise. Jesus knew he needed to give the disciples an empirically solid foundation. That's why he showed them his hands and feet.

Peter and John were later hauled before the council of religious leaders in Jerusalem for teaching that, through Jesus, there was resurrection from the dead (Acts 4:1-20). The members of the council were shocked and amazed at this teaching. They thought it was crazy and commanded the two disciples to stop poisoning the minds of the people with such rubbish. But Peter and John said, "We cannot help speaking about what we have seen and heard" (Acts 4:20). In reporting this exchange, it's as if Luke (the author of Acts) is saying to his readers and to us across the centuries, "I know your worldview says that resurrection is impossible. Ours does too. It was just as stunning to us as it is to you. The only reason I am telling you about it is because it really happened."

Friends, the most rational historical, literary, cultural explanation for the Resurrection is that it really happened. Jesus, the disciples, and all of Scripture address the intellectual roadblocks of doubt, and when we examine the evidence from all angles, it adds up. In fact, to say it didn't happen actually creates more problems and questions. There is no credible evidence from the first century that anyone was able to refute the Resurrection. Hundreds of witnesses all told the same story: "He's alive. I saw him." This is what Luke is getting at, and this is what Jesus was addressing. "Here I am—alive, here."

So we have a choice: Call the disciples liars or believe that Jesus was actually resurrected. But to suggest that the disciples were self-serving conspirators or superstitious neophytes doesn't stand up to scrutiny.

Once you are convinced that the resurrection of Jesus is true, you have a foundation of empirical evidence on which you can build your faith and deal honestly with your doubt. Conversely, any doubt about the reality of God must answer the historical evidence of the resurrection of Christ and debunk him as a charlatan and a liar.

You might say, "I'm not a person of faith. God is not necessary for my life." If that's the case, then intellectual honesty demands that you "doubt your doubts."[6] Ask yourself why you do not feel a need for God. Is it because you are competent to run your own life? What is your basis for believing that? Why doubt faith in God and not doubt faith in yourself? Is that logical or fair?

Is it because you demand control or freedom to live however you want to live? More than a century ago, Philip James Bailey wrote in his poem *Festus*: "[Those] who never doubted, never half believed. Where doubt, there truth is— 'tis her shadow."[7] Look for the truth behind your doubts. Does your rejection of your need for God point to a desire for autonomy in your life? Is that the best way to live? Can anyone really live autonomously? By asking honest, humble, insightful questions like these, we can gain greater clarity about our personal motivations and what must be objectively true for our lives and the world to make any sense. This need to "doubt our doubts" is true for believers and skeptics alike.

Sometimes we think our doubt sets us free from the confining shackles of faith, but that's not true. Every doubt is based on a position of faith. As Timothy Keller writes, "If you doubt Christianity because 'There cannot be just *one* true religion,' you must recognize that this statement is itself an act of faith."[8] Likewise, to say, "'I can't accept the existence of moral absolutes' . . . is [also] a leap of faith" because it is not a universally accepted belief and cannot be empirically proven to someone who disagrees with you.[9] Whether you are a skeptic or a follower of Jesus, faith and doubt always grow in the same garden.

THE MYSTERY OF GOD'S LOVE AND PRESENCE

We are a people who love to have answers—rock solid evidence and closure—not just for what we think but also for what we feel. Unfortunately, believing in God does not give us all the answers. We are not comfortable with mystery, and because mystery surrounds so much of who God is and what he is doing, it can feel as if our faith is not on solid ground. (What good is it to believe in God if we are drowning in questions?) But mystery is part of the fabric of human life.

Everyone experiences mystery on an almost daily basis, but we just accept it and hardly know it is there. We have all heard the stories: the cancer that miraculously disappears before treatment has even begun, the inkling that leads someone to call a friend who lives halfway across the country and is in trouble. In fact, our lives thrive on mystery. We all experience things we know are real—and would bet our lives on—but we can't fully explain, such as the boundless joy of seeing our child for the first time or the surprising transcendence of a mountain sunrise. How can we adequately explain the deep rapture of soul that grips us all from time to time and for different reasons without resorting to the language of mystery? We can't. Many things cannot be fully captured in words, but that does not mean they aren't real. They just have to be experienced to be understood.

The same goes for God. It's not that belief in God is not rational but that it defies rational*ism*. That is, the best theology can explain things *about* God, but it fails to get at the heart of *knowing* God. Knowing God always involves mystery, unanswered questions, and—yes—doubt because the depths of knowing God will never fit into neat theological categories.

I remember the first time I walked into the Notre Dame Cathedral in Paris. I was overwhelmed by the scope and detail of artistry. It is one of the most recognized buildings in the world, and I had seen the pictures and read the guidebooks that explained the architecture and described the art contained in the works of stained glass. But no explanation can do the cathedral justice. It is one thing to read about transcendent architecture and artistic beauty; it is quite another to actually experience them.

Likewise, it is one thing to explain the love of God, but no explanation will be adequate. Understanding involves an engagement of the heart. Again, this does not mean that faith in God or an experience of his love and presence is not rational, it just means that it is not *only* rational. There are (at least) emotional and experiential elements as well, which are equally (if not more) essential to our understanding. Propositions will take us only so far. Love and beauty propel us inevitably into the realm of poetic mystery.

In the Carl Sagan movie *Contact*, a scientist played by

Jodie Foster is propelled into space. She tries to explain the celestial event she is seeing, but cannot. She says, "Poetry! Indescribable . . . they should have sent a poet."

The point is, all of life involves a significant amount of mystery—things we know are real and true but cannot get our minds fully around. Why do we think our experience of God should be any different? Why do we think we should be able to fully understand God or explain him in minute detail in order to justify our faith? Life doesn't work that way.

God has definitively revealed himself and his purposes in the Bible and in creation. But the way he does so is often in poetry, song, visions, and complex beauty. Jesus told parables and used countless metaphors that are shrouded in mystery. Even the intellectual apostle Paul resorts to poetry and mystery language at times in describing faith in God.

The love of a mother for her child, the compassion of a friend, the care of a social worker, the patience of a teacher, even the captivated curiosity of a scientist—these are things of wonder and mystery. Such is life and such is God.

ENTER THE SANCTUARY

Asaph struggles with the vertigo of faith and doubt in Psalm 73. He witnesses suffering and cruelty at the hands of the arrogant who mock God, and yet God seems to do nothing in response. Asaph begins to despair: "Surely in vain I have kept my heart pure and have washed my hands in innocence" (verse 13). Maybe this God stuff is all a sham?

He continues, "When I tried to understand all this, it

troubled me deeply till I entered the sanctuary of God; then I understood" (verses 16-17).

What did he understand?

That God is not only real, he is a God of justice and hope for the oppressed. He is a God who will destroy evil and put things to rights and will not ultimately allow injustice and abuse to win.

We witness suffering, death, broken relationships, cruelty, betrayal, and the bad guys winning, and it breaks our hearts. Our doubts are not purely intellectual. Most often, they have an experiential aspect as well. So we must not only seek intellectual answers to our questions about God, we must seek experiential answers as well. We should bring our *experience* of doubt into God's sanctuary.

Am I saying that we should engage in worshiping God even if we're not sure we believe in him? Yes, absolutely. It's not a fair test otherwise. We must engage more than our intellect; we must connect with the fullness of our emotions—anger, hurt, fear, confusion, hope—as well. We need to sing, even if with a heart of bitterness or cynicism. We need to place ourselves in a position to subjectively engage the presence of God. This is simply the way humans are built. We cannot reasonably expect to know another person without experiencing his or her affection, friendship, affirmation, or correction. I may know hundreds of facts about my favorite actor or singer, but it would be ludicrous to think, having never spent time with either one, that I actually know them. The same goes for God. He is not some cosmic celebrity to be revered from afar. He is a heavenly Father to be experienced and known.

G. K. Chesterton writes, "The Christian ideal has not been tried and found wanting. It has been found difficult, and left untried."[10] It is unfair and dishonest to doubt God—whether as a believer or a skeptic—if we are unwilling to put ourselves in the place where he is found: in the sanctuary of worship, the closet of prayer, and the shared life with fellow children of God.

People aren't merely argued into the faith. There is always an experiential side to doubt that must be dealt with experientially. Relationship with God is not an invitation to have all of our questions answered and the mysteries of life solved. Again, life doesn't work that way. Instead, it is an invitation to know a love and acceptance that transcends all of our foolishness and frailty.

This is the reason our churches must be, or become, places that allow people to encounter God regardless of where they are on their spiritual journey. Engaging God in worship is not just for the spiritually healthy, but for the cynical and broken as well. That is the only way doubt can be fully dealt with. Doubt belongs in the sanctuary, mixed in with our professions of faith. In Christ, God invites us to know him deeply and be shaped by his affection and truth, no matter where we currently find ourselves on the spectrum of cynicism and hope, of faith and doubt. Because of the experiential root of much, if not most, of our doubt, God must be an object of worship, not abstract speculation, if we are to deal with him honestly. Otherwise, we will never find him.

What would Asaph have seen when he entered the sanctuary?

The sanctuary he would have gone to was the Jewish Temple in Jerusalem, and he would have seen sacrifices being offered by the priests. In the book of Hebrews, we learn that these animal sacrifices were made to atone for sin and they foreshadowed the sacrifice of Jesus. The Bible tells us that Jesus' sacrifice on the cross answers all that has gone wrong with the world—sin, oppression, alienation, you name it—and his resurrection inaugurates a Kingdom of peace, a new way to be human. Only in Jesus do we have both an acknowledgment of the world's problems—that this is not the way things are supposed to be—and the solution, that he is putting the world to rights and making all things new.

When you doubt, enter the sanctuary. Remember the sacrifice. Don't run from your doubt. Be honest about it. Allow it to fertilize the soil of faith.

You have a choice. Either you will believe that God is real and has answered the world's problems in Jesus, or you won't. Either way, it requires faith.

CHAPTER 6

PIRATES AND FREAKS
HAVING THE COURAGE TO CHANGE

The boy didn't need to hear it.
There was already a deep, black
wordless conviction in him that the
way to avoid Jesus was to avoid sin.
FLANNERY O'CONNOR, *WISE BLOOD*

Jerry was a freak. Then again, we were in seventh grade; nobody got by unscathed. For most of us, the saving grace that rescued us from the universal prejudice and cruelty of middle school was finding someone to look down on who was more awkward, more uncoordinated, more shunned by the opposite sex than we were.

In my school, that someone was Jerry. He was the unchallenged low man on the totem pole—the pubescent pariah—and everyone knew it. Even he knew it. I wasn't popular, or cool, or athletic, but at least I wasn't Jerry.

One of Jerry's legs was significantly shorter than the other, so he didn't walk, he waddled. He wore one of those shoes with a four-inch sole. Kids joked that it made him look like Frankenstein's monster, tottering and lumbering through the halls.

But the worst part was the smell. In all my twelve years on the planet, I had never whiffed anything like it, and I was convinced that prolonged exposure would shut down my internal organs. Others must have shared my concern, because when Jerry passed us in the halls, it was as if he was surrounded by a repellent magnetic field. Nobody would get within six feet. He was like Moses parting the Red Sea, only this sea was cruel and mocking and unforgiving.

One day I was in the restroom when Jerry came in. The other boys quickly made for the exit, but I was not so lucky, as I was otherwise occupied and unable to retreat. In desperation, I drew in all the fresh oxygen left in the room, wondering which would go first—my liver? kidneys? spleen? (What does that do, anyway?) Can a foul stench cause cancer? Would the air in my lungs be enough to sustain me until I could flee? I wasn't sure, but I had to try. I stood holding my breath and cursing myself for having had that extra carton of milk at lunch.

That was when I saw it.

I noticed that Jerry hadn't approached the urinal in the customary way. He was standing a little sideways and had unbuttoned his shirt from the bottom. *What is he doing?*

In my mind, I was screaming, *Don't look! Don't look!* but curiosity got the best of me and I violated lavatory protocol, glancing quickly in Jerry's direction in an effort to figure out his odd posture.

Jerry had a catheter bag. Of course, I didn't know what

that was at the time. All I knew was that he had a bag full of urine attached to his waist and hidden under his ill-fitting clothing. It looked a lot like one of those bags they use when you're donating blood, only not quite as big. And he was dumping it.

That explained the smell. The sad part was that it wasn't even his fault. Yet the unfortunate and unavoidable aroma made Jerry an outcast in an already alien, unrelenting, and callous middle school universe.

Still holding my breath as if my life depended on it, I wondered for the first time how it must feel to be him—to have literally no friends, to sit alone at lunch every day, to have no one get within six feet at any time. It must be terrible. We were cruel. And all because he looked, and smelled, different from the rest of us.

TOTEM POLES OF PIETY AND POPULARITY

As an adult, I now realize that we still do the same thing in categorizing other people. In theory, we are more mature, understanding, and tolerant. We fancy ourselves as open-minded and inclusive grown-ups who have moved beyond the barbaric and judgmental world of adolescent marginalization of all that is dissimilar to our relative standard of hipness—a standard that is, not surprisingly, crafted in our own image.

Even in the church, we judge and rate people, classifying them according to an often unspoken standard of how Christians are "supposed" to look, speak, and behave. Churchgoers, at a minimum, should be well groomed, with shirts tucked in, teeth brushed, and backs straight. They aren't supposed to smell like lust or question the reality or relevance of God. In a sense, Christians aren't supposed to limp. Those who do may end up sitting alone at the Wednesday night potluck dinner.

Unfortunately, all too often this is the message we send, even among the so-called hip and culturally relevant churches. In communities of faith replete with vintage T-shirts with ironic slogans, trendy jeans, and environmentally sensitive footwear, the arrogance and condescension expressed toward seersucker suits and starched collars, organ music, and fixed pews is often just as palpable and egregious as the disapproval of denim, piercings, and tattoos among more staid congregations.

The dirty little secret is that Christians do smell—and limp. All of us. We act as if we have it all together—hiding our infirmities, fears, and doubts behind memory verses and perfect church attendance, or indie music and haircuts that are supposed to make a cultural statement—all so we won't be the low man on the totem pole of piety or cultural popularity.

But in church, just as in middle school, such relational jockeying is hostile to love. Even worse, it is contrary to the gospel of Jesus Christ.

OWNING OUR LIMP

Why are we so afraid to admit that we walk through our lives with a spiritual limp? Why do we keep others at arm's length, lest they catch a whiff of our moral failures and struggles with faith? Should we really be that concerned that others in the church will reject us if they know we're not like them, that we doubt a lot, that we sin even more, or that our hearts are often incredibly cluttered and unkempt?

We work so hard to present a façade of superior spirituality or obedience or religious diligence, but the performance isn't really for our fellow moralists. The ultimate object of our con job is God.

We assume that God respects our hierarchical flowchart rankings of spiritual superiority. We assume he shares our polite derision of the spiritually weak and lame among us. But he doesn't. Jesus made this clear when he told a parable about a religious snob and a universally despised tax collector who prayed to God. The religious guy said, "God, I thank you that I am not like other people—robbers, evildoers, adulterers." The tax man beat his breast and said, "God, have mercy on me, a sinner" (Luke 18:11, 13). Jesus said only the tax man went away justified before God.

God delights to show up in the lives of the beaten and broken, meeting us in our honest confession of frailty and failure. What should be terrifying to us is that he turns his back on arrogant elitism, whether explicitly verbalized, carefully tucked away in our hearts, or couched in the unspoken cultural expectations of our churches.

We say we believe this, but we act as if it's not true. Meanwhile, we're not only missing the opportunity to see the healing presence of Christ in the diverse lives of people in our cities and neighborhoods, we're also, perhaps unwittingly, missing out on seeing the full transformative power of the gospel in our own hearts. We are mistaken if we assume that as long as there is someone who is a bigger screwup than we are, God will leave us to our petty vices and focus on the other person. If I "smell" just a little better than you or my limp is less obvious, then maybe God will never have to deal with me. Or more accurately, maybe I will never have to deal with God.

It all comes down to the fact that we don't want God to show up in our lives. Put simply, we are afraid to venture into the briarpatch of our own spiritual masquerade because somehow we know God is there, and when God shows up he might start rearranging the spiritual furniture—or worse, he might tell us to get out of the house and start touching the lives of other people. We are afraid to live in his penetrating presence because it will require us to do things like change and repent and forgive and love others as God has loved us. When the presence of God breaks in, it challenges us to see the world, and ourselves, in a different light. And that's scary. It's much easier to keep our masks on and glare reproachfully from a distance at the obvious sinners and religious fugitives in our communities. To maintain our spiritual status quo (however stagnant), we must hide our limps and our catheter bags from others and from God.

But deep down, we *know* we are spiritually crippled and need healing. Our veneer of piety and penance cannot disguise the truth that we are no better than the next person and desperately need God to show up. Paradoxically, the healing presence of God can be painful. When God breaks in, he exposes our arrogance and our failure, our snobbery and our woeful lack of love. When God breaks in, he brings into sharp relief the fact that we walk with a pronounced spiritual limp and need the healing touch of Jesus, who brings the fresh aroma of love, peace, and grace into our lives for all the world to smell (2 Corinthians 2:15).

LET THE HEALING BEGIN

The good news is that we are accepted by God through the life, death, and resurrection of Jesus, in spite of our foolishness and failure. But too often we live more by the imprudent principles of pubescent seventh graders than by the promises of the gospel of grace. Will we have the courage to accept the transformative presence of God in our prickly hearts, or perhaps to actually *seek* it? To seek God's presence is to admit that we limp. We need to be forgiven, to be accepted, to be loved, to be healed, to be given the power to love others, and to follow God together with our fellow fools.

And this is precisely what the curative presence of God brings. We are healed of our fear of failure and of being exposed. In our communities of faith, we are set free from the self-righteousness that allows us to look down our noses at those who are seemingly less spiritual than we are, or those who have never stepped inside a church building.

When healing happens, church becomes more than a *place* where we attend and pretend. The church is once again a people, among whom acceptance and grace are palpable, because we are finally able to admit that we—all of us—are people being restored by the life, death, and resurrection of Jesus. Churches become gathering places where those who don't know God are able to come and not have to hold their breath for fear of ingesting the stench of self-righteousness.

Or better yet, the people of God break out of the confines of our buildings and meetings and permeate our neighborhoods, workplaces, and schools with the healing and hopeful aroma of Christ in everyday life. Friends, this is not just a possibility; it is what we are called to do.

The gospel story is one that breaks into our lives indiscriminately and brings a much-needed objectivity. Whether we are Pharisees or tax collectors, the message is the same. Jesus says, "My beloved, I came for you. I see all the spiritual stuff you do and that's really cute and all, but I know you're still a mess. You may try to hide it from everyone else, but I know. And when you start to really believe that I make you a beloved child of God in spite of your foolishness, then you'll stop minding so much if everyone else knows your faults." The grace and acceptance of God that is given to us in Christ frees us up so that we can finally see ourselves in relation to God's presence in our lives, rather than in comparison to one another. We don't care if they smell and limp because we're all smelly and limping! The presence of God is the death knell to spiritual posturing and the soil in which real transformation begins to grow, if only we have the courage to go there.

GETTING NAKED

Eustace, the protagonist in C. S. Lewis's *The Voyage of the "Dawn Treader,"* is an absolute beast of a boy—nasty, mean-spirited, and spiteful. He discovers a dragon's treasure and decides it is his for the taking. After falling asleep on the treasure, he awakens to find he has become on the outside what he was on the inside—a dragon. No longer is his folly hidden; in essence his heart has been exposed. Now everyone can see his corruption and foolishness. And he's devastated.

Aslan the lion, the Christ figure in the story, appears and takes Eustace to a refreshing well of water. "You can get in, but you have to undress first," Aslan says. It seems like a great offer, so Eustace agrees. Meticulously peeling off the scales and dragon skin, Eustace steps to the edge of the water only to see his reflection on the smooth surface and realize the dragon skin is still there. Not one to give up easily, he tries two more times but with the same result.

Finally Aslan says, "You will have to let me undress you." As the lion's claws begin to pierce his skin, Eustace realizes that Aslan is going much deeper than expected, far beyond the surface layer.

> "The very first tear . . . was so deep that I thought it had gone right into my heart. . . . It hurt worse than anything I've ever felt. The only thing that made me able to bear it was just the pleasure of feeling the stuff peel off. . . .
>
> "Then he caught hold of me—I didn't like that much for I was very tender underneath now that I'd no skin on—and threw me into the water. It smarted like anything but only for a moment. After that it became perfectly delicious and as soon as I started swimming and splashing I found that . . . I'd turned into a boy again. . . . After a bit the lion took me out and dressed me." . . .
>
> The cure had begun.[1]

This is the healing that happens when God shows up and meets us in the briarpatch—the prickly places deep within our hearts. The healing is often painful because it requires both exposure and peeling. When we're exposed in the presence of God, we can no longer hide our faults and failings, and somehow we find that we don't really want to anymore. We find a surprising freedom and joy in being spiritually naked before God and others as our scales of idolatry, pride, arrogance, and self-righteousness are peeled away. Because we have often spent years growing, perfecting, and placing these scales, having them taken off feels very much like picking off a not-quite-healed scab. The healing hurts, which is why we all try very hard to keep it from happening. It is much easier to keep up our religious façades, telling ourselves—and God—that we are just fine, thank you very much.

But hiding behind religious façades turns us into deluded "dragons" engaged in a macabre dance of deception with one another, all the while assuming that nobody notices our scales or limp. This charade has utterly infected the so-called Christian culture, and I'm not sure if we should laugh at the sheer lunacy of it or cry because we are missing out on *so much*. Either way, it's pathetic. Everyone is afraid to be the first one to get naked, to expose the raw skin underneath. For as much as we talk about our freedom in Christ, few of us are brave enough to get peeled (and healed). It takes real courage.

Let me be honest. I don't have this all figured out. I'm no expert. I'm an idiot. I struggle to allow the claws of God's mercy to dig deeply into my heart, and I am sure you do too. But will we have the courage to admit, maybe for the first time, that we need the presence of God to pierce our souls and change us on the inside, not just the outside?

Here's what I do know: The gospel is equally for the self-righteous and the self-loathing. The life, death, and resurrection of Jesus on our behalf *should* set us free from needing to commend ourselves to God and others (and even to ourselves). When we truly understand what Jesus did on our behalf, there's no longer any need for posturing or comparing because we all come to God together—smells, limps, scales, and all.

And when we finally get it—when we finally grasp the full truth of the gospel—we begin to see all those other jerks and weirdos and losers through the same lens of mercy and grace that God sees us. We realize that if God can love *us*, he can love them, too. Or looking at it from the other side, if God *cannot* love them, there's no hope for us. The presence of God changes our hearts, and it usually hurts because there's a lot of crud that has to be peeled away. And we can't do it for ourselves. All we can do is surrender to the waters of God's mercy. And surrender we must, even as we invite our friends and neighbors to join us.

CHANGE OF PERSPECTIVE

David the Pirate was homeless and had been for fifteen years or so. He was not really a pirate, but the kids thought he looked like one because of his scraggly beard, raspy voice, and the slew of faded tattoos collected during his days in the US Merchant Marine. Suffice it to say, David spent a lot of time with Jim Beam and Johnnie Walker, and the remnants and aroma of this fellowship often lingered into Sunday morning. Between his gregarious personality, the smell of whiskey, and his lack of regular access to a shower or a washing machine, the Pirate did not go unnoticed at our church. Yet somehow he fit in. One time he even volunteered to help pass out worship guides to folks as they came into the service. That didn't last long because the worship guides fell out of his hands, and as he dropped them, he simultaneously dropped the F-bomb—repeatedly and loudly.

We found him another job out of earshot of small children.

At any rate, David the Pirate usually sat in the back. I'm not sure why. Maybe he thought he didn't belong in the front. One Sunday, as the sermon was wrapping up and we were going into prayer, he made his way forward, knelt at the front of our stage, bowed his head, and began sobbing. A few people (who had recently bathed and had not, to my knowledge, dropped the F-bomb in church) gathered around David, put their arms around him, and quietly prayed with him. A few minutes later, as we began the Eucharist liturgy, in a quiet moment and with impeccable timing, David the Pirate looked up at me with tears streaming down his dirty face, and in a loud voice that sounded like a chain-smoking Popeye, said, "Pastor, the gospel is kicking my ass!"

After a moment of shocked silence at the breach of our normal decorum, we laughed and cheered, celebrating the healing presence of Jesus among us. It was one of the most redemptive moments I have ever witnessed.

Not everyone cheered, of course, and I'm sure some

thought the whole thing was inappropriate and offensive to God. Even though it came from a redemptive piercing deep in David the Pirate's soul, many would see his eruption as an unwelcome and crass interruption of the solemnity and holiness of the Eucharist. But such is life in the briarpatch, among the uncouth and even repulsive, where Jesus calls us to go with his grace. It can feel prickly to welcome folks like this into our lives, especially into our times of worship. But this is where Jesus shows up and people are changed—perhaps even you and me.

One person's celebration can be a burr under the saddle to someone else. That happens in the Bible, too. In Luke 15:1-7, Jesus tells the parable of the Lost Sheep.

> Now the tax collectors and sinners were all gathering around to hear Jesus. But the Pharisees and the teachers of the law muttered, "This man welcomes sinners and eats with them." Then Jesus told them this parable: "Suppose one of you has a hundred sheep and loses one of them. Doesn't he leave the ninety-nine in the open country and go after the lost sheep until he finds it? And when he finds it, he joyfully puts it on his shoulders and goes home. Then he calls his friends and neighbors together and says, 'Rejoice with me; I have found my lost sheep.' I tell you that in the same way there will be more rejoicing in heaven over one sinner who repents than over ninety-nine righteous persons who do not need to repent."

You see, religion tells us that God wants good people, so we do all we can to be good, if not on the inside, at least on the outside. But Jesus says that God wants *new* people. He wants the uncouth former merchant marine just as much as he wants buttoned-down accountants. He welcomes limping sinners into his healing and sometimes painful presence. And so a Pirate and a Pharisee alike can stand in the presence of God with boldness and impunity because the invitation comes from God himself. If we only have the courage to come.

I have begun to realize that the difference between David the Pirate and me is a matter of perspective. Clearly, I am more adept than he is at things like using a toothbrush, holding down a job, and knowing not to drop the F-bomb in polite company. Based on outward appearances, I am safely entrenched in my fortress of superiority. But does such a perspective even exist in the economy of God?

The Bible says that God rejoices when anyone comes to him in faith and repentance, whether that person uses deodorant or not. But we don't like this liberal inclusivity because it exposes the shaky foundation of our self-righteousness and threatens our perch of religious superiority. When we acknowledge that someone who is so far outside of respectable society or religion is actually on equal footing with us before the Cross, our religious pretensions begin to vanish. We suddenly find ourselves naked before Jesus and others. It can be terribly uncomfortable, but the presence of God both *pierces* and *heals* us, if we have the courage to surrender control of our lives to God. Before God, we stand side by side with the pirates, freaks, and Pharisees because really we are all the same. We are all broken and need the messy and mysterious presence of God.

We might think it would be much easier if *real* sinners would just stay away from our religious gatherings. But then, if we're honest, we would have to stay away too. It takes courage to live in the prickly, piercing, transforming presence of God because it takes courage to change.

INTO THE
BRIARPATCH

CHAPTER 7

FOLLOWING THE STORY
CAN SUCH AN OLD BOOK EVER LEAD THE WAY?

There is no greater agony than bearing an untold story inside you.

MAYA ANGELOU

When we learn to read the story of Jesus and see it as the story of the love of God, doing for us what we could not do for ourselves—that insight produces, again and again, a sense of astonished gratitude which is very near the heart of authentic Christian experience.

N. T. WRIGHT

When I was in school, I had to read many works of literature that were confusing, dark, and hard to read. Among them was Charles Dickens's *Great Expectations*. It described a world foreign to my modern and middle-class experience—escaped convicts, mysterious mansions, and secret benefactors. At such a young age, relating to the world and events described in *Great Expectations* proved to be an exasperating challenge.

For many of us, the Bible proves to be equally difficult,

especially early on in our lives of faith. The stories are of strange nations and past civilizations, of people who practiced bizarre customs and lived lives that could scarcely be more foreign to our own, with polygamous and murderous kings, genocide that seems to be sanctioned by God, rituals of sacrifice, a calamitous flood, and miracles that defy scientific explanation. It can feel as if we've wandered into an obscure, bleak, alien world that is hard to even understand, much less use to guide our lives and faith in the modern day.

One of the more famous scenes in *Great Expectations* finds Pip, the protagonist, visiting the house of Miss Havisham for the first time. The house "was of old brick, and dismal, and had a great many iron bars to it. Some of the windows had been walled up; of those that remained, all the lower were rustily barred."[1] It was old, dark, foreboding, and uninviting.

The inside of the house proves to be just as gloomy and strange as it was on the outside. Pip continues, "We went into the house by a side door—the great front entrance had two chains across it outside—and the first thing I noticed was that the passages were all dark, and that she had left a candle burning there. . . . We went through more passages and up a staircase, and still it was all dark, and only the candle lighted us."[2]

Once inside, the darkness and confusion seem to grow. What kind of a place is this? The scene inspires more questions than it provides answers. And it only gets weirder.

Pip finally meets Miss Havisham, the lady of the house, who had been jilted on her wedding day many years before, and it is one of the oddest scenes in all of literature. She is still wearing her wedding dress, the clocks are all stopped at twenty minutes to nine—the time of her rejection—and a wedding feast is set at the table.

> I saw that everything within my view which ought
> to be white, had been white long ago, and had lost
> its lustre, and was faded and yellow. I saw that the
> bride within the bridal dress had withered like the
> dress, and like the flowers, and had no brightness
> left but the brightness of her sunken eyes. I saw that
> the dress had been put upon the rounded figure of
> a young woman, and that the figure upon which it
> now hung loose, had shrunk to skin and bone.[3]

There is a story contained in this house that begs to be told—of lives and events not fully explained or easily understood, yet that are rich with meaning and would have direct implications for the direction of Pip's life.

When we meet God and begin to read the Bible seriously, many of us are like Pip—walking into a house once alive that now feels dark, dull, irrelevant, and lifeless. The Bible often strikes us as cluttered with the cobwebs of outdated writing and irrelevant stories. It is an often confusing grab bag of poetry, history, folktales, and ethical instruction that seem to be stuck in a time warp.

But someone has left a candle burning in the hallway.

Then something moves and we get the sense there is life stirring—maybe there's a story to be told. Maybe there is hope and life to be discovered here after all, if we would pick up the candle and begin to make our way down the hall. And as we walk, we find ourselves being shaped by the stories and events—equipped and encouraged to live lives of purpose and meaning that would otherwise have been lost to us.

TRAJECTORY OF HOPE

Is the story of the Bible foundationally one of hope? I would say yes. Behind and beneath the misdeeds and misdirection of God's people lies a definitive thread of redemption and healing. If you are a follower of God, that thread runs through your life as well. You are part of the story.

When I was young, I used to love spending the night at my grandmother's house. I always awoke in the morning to the smell of homemade biscuits baking in the oven and sausage gravy simmering on the stove. She always had her kitchen radio tuned to the gospel music station, and the old hymns reverberated off the metal cabinets and plastered walls.

I had very little interest in spiritual things back then, but I was struck by the joy with which my grandmother sang along to hymns like "Beulah Land" and "When the Roll Is Called Up Yonder." With lyrics that spoke of a "home beyond the skies" and taking our "heavenly flight," those songs had a decided focus on the eventual escape of this world and all its troubles—a focus that is understandable, but entirely wrong.

What did Jesus mean when he said, "When you clothed the naked, cared for the sick, or fed the hungry, you did this for me" (Matthew 25:40, my paraphrase)? Is he saying that we literally gave him food or clothing or that the person in need was somehow a manifestation of Christ's presence among us? No, I don't think so. What he meant was that our actions of compassion and healing are an integral part of his purposes for the world. It is shorthand for our participation in God's central theme of hope—his intention to put the world to rights.

This is the story that Christians desperately need to rediscover—the overarching biblical assertion that God is not done with this world, but rather loves it and intends to *renew* it. The Bible's trajectory of hope, which culminates in the death and resurrection of Jesus, militates against the idea that God will wipe his hands of this world and so must we.

But you might say, "Aren't we told that our citizenship is in heaven?" (see Philippians 3:20). Well, yes, we are. But Paul says we are waiting for our Savior to *return* from there and bring everything under his control and make us like him (see Philippians 3:20-21). There is no talk of destroying the earth or of our escaping the world. The Philippians to whom Paul wrote would have understood this. Many of them were Roman citizens—their citizenship was in Rome—but that did not mean they were expecting to end up in Italy when they retired. Their role as citizens was to bring Roman culture to bear in the city of Philippi.

And that is the point of our role as citizens of heaven and our participation in God's story of hope that finds its climax in the resurrection of Jesus. Jesus rose from the dead; therefore, God's new world of life, hope, and renewal has broken in to our world of corruption, sin, and death. Jesus rose from the dead, and those who share in his resurrection life have a new job to do: to bring the life of heaven to this world in actual, physical, earthly reality.

That is the reality to which all of Scripture points. It is the entire reason Jesus came—not just to save our souls, but to restore our world and bring his Kingdom of grace and peace to rule on earth. That's why he taught us to pray, "Your kingdom come, your will be done, on earth as it is in heaven" (Matthew 6:10). In other words, "God, help us to make heaven more of a reality here on earth," in anticipation of the full renewal that is coming and that is reflected in the promise of Jesus in Revelation 21:5: "I am making everything new!"

We stand against injustice because God hates injustice. We care for the environment because God made the world, loves the world, has called it good, and has made us stewards of it. That is the story of God in the Bible, and it is our story. We work against systems of poverty, marginalization, and abuse that are inherent in our political, social, and economic structures because God's story in the Bible is one with a trajectory of hope and healing for the world. His intention is to bring the rule and reign of Jesus to bear over every facet of his creation.

The life, death, and resurrection of Jesus is not our ticket *out* of the world; it is our commission of hope *to* the world. The resurrected Jesus is the prototype of the world as it will be and has already begun to be. It is the continuation of the trajectory of hope that we are invited to participate in and help cultivate. God has given us the privilege and responsibility to model his Kingdom now and to bring a taste of what his reign will ultimately be.

But even if we understand what the Bible says, how can we be sure it is a true and trustworthy guide for us as we enter the briarpatch?

TRUSTWORTHY AND TRUE?

Belief in the Bible as the revelation of God—our guide for life with God and others—has always been a central tenet of the Christian faith. But such a belief is a stumbling block for many who wonder, "How can I trust the Bible? There are so many things in there that are confusing, culturally regressive, contradictory, or just plain wrong." So much of what is contained in the Bible is viewed as irrelevant at best, and probably harmful to life in the modern world.

As we begin to consider what it looks like to walk into the briarpatch, we must consider the role of the Bible in guiding our way. Can we trust the Bible?

In college, when I first came to faith in Jesus, there was a tacit acceptance of the Bible's authority in the lives of Christians. It was read publicly and privately. I was encouraged to memorize parts of it, and we studied it in church and in our weekly gatherings. The more I read of it, the more it made sense, but that's not saying much. There were vast sections that beautifully described the pursuing love of God and the sacrifice of Jesus for the sins of the world. That was all well and good; but what about all the other stuff—the leaders of God's people who had sex with their own children, killed their siblings, and seemed to have no problem wiping out entire nations, including women and children? How come we never studied that stuff in church? I was told that the Bible was the authoritative Word of God, but I was never given a cogent reason for such a belief.

The authority of Scripture was just assumed. And to be honest, I was fine with that assumption. I figured I had a lot to learn, and for the time being, the church's historic acceptance of the Bible's authority was good enough for me. But I knew that would not always be enough. My questions would eventually need to be at least partially answered. So I began a slow and patient search for answers that continues to this day. There are many parts of the Bible I still do not understand, and there are things I still find objectionable and embarrassing, but I do believe the Bible to be a sufficient and clear guide for my everyday life.

How did I come to that conviction?

The process of discerning whether or not we can trust the Bible begins with the question of its *historicity*. Is the Bible historically reliable? Some critics assert that it is religious legend or myth, with no basis in actual history. C. S. Lewis was professor of Medieval and Renaissance English at Oxford for nearly thirty years. He was also a Christian. In response to the assertion that the Bible, particularly the four Gospels, was something other than historically reliable, he wrote, "I have been reading poems, romances, vision-literature, legends, myths all my life. I know what they are like. I know that not one of them is like this. . . . Either [the Gospels are] reportage . . . pretty close up to the facts . . . or else some unknown writer in the second century, without known predecessors or successors, suddenly anticipated the whole technique of modern, novelistic, realistic narrative.

. . . The reader who doesn't see this has simply not learned to read."[4]

In other words, Lewis is saying, "I know what ancient myth or legend is, and this ain't it." We can know that the story of the Bible tells us what basically really happened. And if we investigate what the Bible says—particularly the New Testament—this position makes sense for a number of reasons (which we can only touch on here).

First, at the time the New Testament was written, there were still a great number of living eyewitnesses—Christian, Jewish, and secular—to the life and ministry of Jesus. The New Testament writers base their accounts on eyewitness testimony and their own experience (see, for example, Luke 1:1-4 and 1 John 1:1-3). They name specific people who saw Jesus perform miracles and could vouch for the veracity of what the writer was saying. In 1 Corinthians 15, Paul appeals to several witnesses of the Resurrection, "most of whom are still living" (verse 6). The religious and political leaders of the time had great motivation to try to debunk the claims surrounding Jesus, but there is no evidence, either in first-century popular or historical writing, of anyone ever succeeding.

Second, Jesus' silence on controversial issues of the first-century church is curious. The best example of this is the dispute over circumcision that divided Christians at the time of the writing of the New Testament. Was a follower of Jesus required to be circumcised? It was a huge disagreement that occupied a significant amount of the early church's time and energy. Yet—and this is where it is important for our purposes here—in every instance where this controversy is addressed in the New Testament, no one refers to any words of Jesus on the topic. Why? Because Jesus didn't directly address the issue—at least not in the company of anyone the writers knew—and they therefore did not feel the liberty to put words in his mouth. So the accusation that the writers of the New Testament made stuff up to serve their own agenda just doesn't hold water. If they were driven by an agenda, rather than by a concern for an accurate account, one or the other side would most assuredly have put words in Jesus' mouth about circumcision. Instead, the silence is deafening.

Third, and perhaps most convincing for me, is all the crazy stuff in the Bible. I believe there is a clear and coherent thread of redemption throughout the Bible, but what about all the salacious tangents and counterproductive cul-de-sacs? Why are we told that the ancestry of Jesus included prostitutes, adulterers, and murderers? Why are we told things that create theological conundrums for us, such as when Jesus' faith seemed to waver in the garden of Gethsemane, just prior to his crucifixion, and he cried out to God and essentially said, "I don't want to do this!" or when he asked God on the cross, "Why have you forsaken me?" Why are we given a picture of the disciples that is less than flattering—petty, jealous, impetuous, and ambitious? The assertion that the Bible, particularly the New Testament, was written to advance a religious agenda or was motivated by a power play on the part of Jesus' disciples makes no sense. If that's what the writers intended, they really screwed it up. If I were writing the New Testament, I would want to present the disciples in the best possible light and would seek to cover up character flaws and spiritual blemishes. Wouldn't you? But the men and women who were leaders of God's people throughout the biblical story are consistently portrayed as flawed and faithless. Why include such troublesome and distracting details unless they are true and accurate depictions?

Luke says, "Since I myself have carefully investigated everything from the beginning, I . . . decided to write an orderly account . . . , so that you may know the certainty of the things you have been taught" (Luke 1:3-4). This is not the language of myth or legend. Whether or not you agree with the meaning of the story of the Bible, to say that it is a fictitious account made up by people who wanted you to believe that Jesus was something he was not just doesn't hold up intellectually or historically.

So the Bible is a historically reliable narrative and is most accurately read as such. It tells a story that is true and reliable, but it is a story nonetheless, which brings us to another issue.

A PEOPLE-SHAPING STORY

Although my children are long past the toddler stage, they still enjoy hearing stories from their early years. They will say, "Tell me about when I was a baby," and Carrie and I will regale them with tales of when they vomited or broke wind during prayer at church or loudly commented on the size of a woman's backside at the mall.

When they ask to hear their story, they're not looking for mere facts and statistics: "You were eight pounds, six ounces, twenty-one inches long, and born at 7:15 in the evening." They don't want to hear that I was working the graveyard shift or that Mom was teaching piano. They want to hear stories of how they baptized their room with baby powder or created the invisible and lethal "dangerous fork" and tried to hold us all hostage.

Perhaps most important, they want to hear how cute they were, how much we loved them from the first time we saw them, and how we used to hold them in the middle of the night for hours on end. They want to hear stories about the things that give them a sense of place in our family's narrative or give them insight into who they are.

We all want to know our own stories. We want to know real things, true things, even literal things about our history, but we learn them best in the context of a narrative that draws us in. This is the way story works, and it is the way the Bible works too.

The biblical story is full of things that we can, and should, take literally—for example, the historical narratives in the Old Testament and the Gospel narratives and letters in the New Testament. But the Bible also contains a significant amount of poetry, song, prophecy, and apocalyptic literature. We read of dragons and sea monsters, rocks crying out, and trees clapping their hands. Parables were one of Jesus' favorite pedagogical tools; and though they're not "true" in the sense that they literally happened, they do truly communicate something about God's love, mercy, Kingdom, etc. Many parts of Scripture were never meant to be taken literally, but rather to paint a picture, communicate the truths of God, and draw us into the story—the true story—of God's care and salvation of the world.

To force the entire Bible through the grid of literalism is to miss the point.

Though the Bible is historically reliable, it is not always "history" per se. It contains many commands, but it cannot be reduced to a rule book. The Bible reveals many truths about God, Jesus, and the world, but it is not merely a doctrinal compendium. The Bible is best described as a complex, interwoven story.

We can get so caught up in propositional summaries or theological proof-texting that we miss the story the Bible is telling about the God who loves and is redeeming the world he has made. When we focus on mining the Scriptures for doctrinal nuggets or rules for religious living, we suck the life out of it. God could have given us a list of commands or propositional truths that would have been far simpler and shorter than the Bible we have. But he didn't. Why? Because that would not capture our hearts like a story does. It would not draw us into the narrative of God's redemption or encourage us to find our meaning and place within that story. God does not just want us to know about what he did, is doing, and will do. He wants us to *participate* in his unfolding drama of redemption—to see that his story is also our story.

The Bible is the story of how God has unleashed his sovereign grace on the world through his people—first Israel in the Old Testament and now the church in the New Testament and beyond. It is the story of how God has revealed himself to his people, guided them, rebuked them when they've gone astray, forgiven them when they've repented, and reminded them of their purpose and calling. Scripture was never intended to impart mere information; it was written less to inform and more to shape the lives of God's children as the conduits of his call and promise to the world.

The Bible, as the authoritative story of God's relationship with humanity, is essential to our having an intimate relationship with God. Often, the distance or indifference we feel with God is due, at least in part, to our not taking the Bible seriously.

The description in Luke 24 of the two men on the road to Emmaus who encounter the resurrected Jesus illustrates this point well. The men were returning from Jerusalem, where the whole city was buzzing because Jesus had been crucified. Jesus met them on the road and said, "What are you talking about?"

Incredulous, they responded, "Dude, where have you been that you don't know what has happened in Jerusalem? We had hoped that Jesus was the redeemer, but he went and got himself crucified." That's my loose paraphrase, but you get the idea.

Then, beginning with Moses and all the Prophets, Jesus explained to them everything the Scriptures said concerning himself. He took them back through the authoritative story of God to show them that this latest event was simply the next chapter of the unfolding of God's purposes in history.

Arriving home, the two men finally recognized Jesus, and he disappeared from their sight. They said, "Were not our hearts burning within us while he talked with us on the road and opened the Scriptures to us?" (Luke 24:32). The word for *heart* here means more than just "the seat of emotions," like we might understand it to mean today. For these disciples, it involved the entirety of their being. So a "burning heart" meant that they had experienced a holistic, overwhelming desire and compulsion for someone or something. This experience of seeing Jesus in the story of Scripture was utterly life-changing. When they understood what it really meant, they felt a love they didn't know was possible, an intimacy they had never imagined, and a connection with God that went to the core of their being. The story engulfed their experience, gave meaning and purpose to their lives, lit their souls on fire, and drew them nearer to God. It will do the same for you and me if we let it.

THE HAND OF GOD

I don't remember how old I was the first time my father took me with him to run errands in downtown Nashville, but I was young enough to be scared and too old to admit it.

I had seen the tall buildings from a distance and wondered what a strange place that must be. So when my father asked if I wanted to go with him to run an errand downtown, I quickly jumped on board.

I was wide-eyed and craned my neck as we turned down Broadway. The buildings towered overhead and seemed to curve and bow politely toward the street.

What kind of people live here? I wondered. *And where do they play baseball or ride go-carts?* I felt sad for the nameless throng, but my sadness quickly gave way to fear as the bars and strip clubs came into view. Their doors were opened wide to the streets, and music punched its way past the men spilling out onto the sidewalk and the women in skirts way too short and heels way too tall.

Why are there pictures of nearly naked women in the windows? Where is there a McDonald's—preferably with a PlayPlace? And why is that man wearing a trench coat in the heat of summer and pushing a grocery cart?

It seemed I was the only one who noticed him shuffling his cart into an alley. One wheel was broken and it strained under the weight of dirty blankets, shapeless scraps of metal, beer bottles, and a tennis racket with broken strings.

His matted beard was the bushiest I had ever seen and was obviously an ecosystem unto itself. My dad had a beard, too, but it was always neatly trimmed. I wondered if this wrinkled and stooped creature was somebody's dad too.

We drove past more shops, bars, restaurants, and places that were boldly marked "Adults Only." We drove past lots and lots of people. Many were in a big hurry and some were shouting at what seemed to be nobody in particular. There were more grocery carts, too.

I had just about had enough and was ready to go back to the familiar safety of the suburbs when we turned into a small parking lot. My father shut off the car and said, "Let's go."

"Huh?" *He actually expects me to go out there!?*

He opened his door and got out.

"I'll wait here." *Thank you very much.*

"Son, let's go." My father is not one who takes kindly to defiance of any kind, so against my better judgment, I opened the door and stepped out into this strange and perilous foreign land.

No sooner had I reached the back of the car than I reached out and took my father's hand. He didn't say anything. He just smiled, as if to say, "I'm here. I've got you," and we were off to run our errand.

The buildings still towered overhead and I had no idea where we were going. I still could make no sense of the amalgam of sights, sounds, and smells that engulfed me. I was afraid and confused, but knew I would be all right.

I'm here. I've got you.

My father knew the way and would guide me. He had a hold on me, so I was safe.

As we encounter the often strange and confusing aspects of our society—the ones that don't fit a Sunday school definition of life—we may feel disoriented, overwhelmed, and out of place. And then we hear God say, "Let's go," and we know it's time to step out in faith and follow as he leads us into the briarpatch.

The Bible gives us a narrative that both guides and guards our steps. That story is the candle that lights our way, defines our world, and reminds us who we are. As we move forward into unexpected and unsettling places, we hold firmly to the hand of God and need not fear the mystery and mess around us. We can have courage to follow Jesus into the thorns and thistles because he says, "I'm here. I've got you" (Matthew 28:20, my paraphrase).

So let's go.

CHAPTER 8

MOVING TOWARD THE RUBBLE
MEETING GOD IN HURRICANES AND THE HOMELESS

Rats and roaches live by competition under
the law of supply and demand; it is the
privilege of human beings to live under the
laws of justice and mercy.

WENDELL BERRY, "ECONOMY AND PLEASURE"

Compassion: that sometimes fatal capacity for
feeling what it is like to live inside another's
skin and for knowing that there can never
really be peace and joy for any until there
is peace and joy finally for all.

FREDERICK BUECHNER, *LISTENING TO YOUR LIFE*

Mr. Buford was sixty-three years old and homeless. He also
was my neighbor and became my friend. A sinewy black
man with sparkling eyes and a toothless grin, he weighed
no more than 110 pounds but was strong as an ox. With an
infectious laugh, he delighted to flex his biceps as proof of
his continued usefulness and vigor. In a street fight, I would
have wanted Mr. Buford on my side.

Except for the seventeen years he spent in prison for a

double homicide, Mr. Buford had lived on our street with his wife and mother for pretty much all his life. When I met him in the fall of 2004, he had lost his wife to cancer, his mother to Alzheimer's, and his home to the underhanded scheming of his niece. The daughter of his late brother took advantage of her grandmother's confused mental state and tricked her into signing away the house. When Mr. Buford's mother died, he was promptly removed from the only home he had ever really known. Unable to bring himself to leave the street on which he had lived for so many decades, he slept on back porches or under bushes when he didn't have the money for bus fare to the shelter downtown.

Mr. Buford would mow your grass, rake your leaves, clean out your gutters, or even help you paint your house. He would help tidy up your garage or plant flowers and carry off lawn debris. If you needed a ladder, he knew someone from whom he could borrow one. He knew everybody, after all. All he asked for in return was something to eat, a cold beer if you had one, and three dollars for the round-trip to the shelter that night.

He was also our one-man neighborhood watch, who took pride in looking out for his friends. He thwarted at least one burglary while the owners were on vacation and exposed a cheating wife whose husband traveled on business. Very little escaped his watchful eye and he would not put up with any nonsense on his street. One night, sometime after midnight, Mr. Buford saw two young men rolling a charcoal grill down the street. It looked exactly like the one on the front porch of a house just across from ours. He hurried to see if the neighbor's grill was still on their porch. It was not. He then chased down the two men, who were probably a third of his age, and wrestled the grill away from them before returning it to its proper place. All was well in the jurisdiction of Mr. Buford.

One evening as we sat on my porch and watched the sun go down, I asked, "So why were you in prison?"

"I kill't two men," he said.

I had expected robbery or even assault, but *murder*? He didn't seem capable. Regardless, he now had my attention.

"Really? You? Was it self-defense?" I asked.

"Naw. I set 'em up."

I had to hear this. "Why would you do something like that?"

"You know that store up over there?" He pointed south. I knew the store well. It's where I stop to get gas and a gallon of milk. "Used to be where pushers and thugs hung out. My wife was up there gettin' cigarettes one night. Two dudes dragged her behind the store and raped her.

"I went up there the next day to shoot dice so I could find out who done it. They was up there and them fools was talking about it, so I acted all friendly to them and we said we was gonna get messed up together. Next day was payday, so we said we would meet up and get us some hits.

"I took Momma's gun with me. We bought some stuff and was walkin' down the street to go get messed up. I was walkin' behind them, and I took my gun and shot one of them. *BLAM!*"

He said it so loud that I jumped.

"The other turned around and I shot him, too. I throwed the gun over in the grass and laid down and waited for the police. Told the police, 'Yeah, I shot 'em with that gun over there.' Judge told me he might've done the same thing if he was me. But he give me seventeen years, and I done every one of 'em.

"But I got saved in prison. I was a changed man. Read my Bible and prayed every day. I know my Bible. You a preacher, so you know the Bible, too, but I know what God says. I don't do drugs no more or gamble or nothin' like that. But I still likes a cold drink sometimes."

Mr. Buford could quote vast sections of Scripture—King James Version—and would often do so during our long talks. He taught me a great deal about what it looks like to know the mercy and forgiveness of God. He knew about grace better than anyone I had ever met. It made my own struggles with lust or anger look like child's play.

"Ain't no difference 'tween you and me, Mr. Shayne," he said. "God loves us both the same. That's how he does. I *know* he loves me. I know it deep. I been livin' on the street for three or four years now, but got everything I need. I ain't hungry. I got clothes and strength. And I got people like you and Miss Carrie lookin' out for me. God is with me. I'm blessed. Yes, sir. I'm blessed and I know it."

Mr. Buford was a reality check for me. I saw him every day for three years, and his presence in my life was a constant reminder that the richness I enjoyed by having a wife and three children who loved me, and a home to live in, and plenty of food to eat was not to be taken for granted. But this was only the beginning of my education at the feet of Mr. Buford.

Our friendship broke through the traditional barriers of age, race, and social class. He was nearly old enough to be my grandfather, and yet we spoke as friends. He was a black man who had lived through the turmoil of segregation in the South, yet he did not hold me guilty for the sins of my Caucasian forebearers. But we didn't hide from our racial differences. I tried to explain to him why white people like to get a tan in the summer, and he told me all about the process of cooking "chitlins," which are pig intestines. I was a pastor with an advanced theological degree, but Mr. Buford would not hesitate to take issue with my understanding of a particular passage or idea about God. Even the gap between our economic situations was of no consequence to our friendship. I came to depend on him as much as he did on me.

He taught me the simple joy of knowing the real affection of God. He showed me that I, too, am blessed. Yes, sir. I'm blessed and I know it.

Eventually, Mr. Buford developed cancer and a heart condition. He would get dizzy and have to rest more often. We tried to get him to go into a home or someplace where he would be more comfortable, but he just couldn't bring himself to leave his street.

Trips to the doctor became more frequent, and he began to talk more about his death. Through tears, he expressed his concern that he had nobody to take care of things when he died. I wrote down all of my contact information and he carried that paper in his pocket, designating me as the person to contact in the event of his death. I promised him that I would make sure he received a proper burial.

Then, one day he didn't come by. Days passed and I never saw him again. I never had the opportunity to make good on my promise. I never received a call. I asked around and nobody knew what happened to my friend. I never found an obituary in the paper. It was as if he vanished.

Not everyone gets to have a friend like Mr. Buford. Not everyone gets to experience the deep affection of God through eyes so different from their own, and thus be blessed to the degree I was. Perhaps he was the kind of friend that comes along only once in a lifetime, but I hope not.

THE DISTRACTION OF MERCY

Most of us go through our lives with no more exposure to homeless people than the occasional pitiful souls camped out at intersections with corrugated placards advertising their desire to work for food or bus fare to a theoretically better place and brighter tomorrow. On a good day, we might give them a few dollars or whatever change happens to be in the ashtray, but mostly we avert our eyes and keep the windows rolled up. Their plight does not penetrate the sanctum of our cars, much less our lives. We simply don't have time, or the stomach, for suffering.

In Decatur, if you walk west from the Avondale subway stop, our church is the first one you come to—about a block away. As a result, we get a lot of walk-in traffic, of people looking for help, and we have to sift through stories of need and desperation. After many years of doing this, our staff has become more adept at discerning between an honest need and a desire for money to score drugs or buy a bottle of cheap wine.

One winter morning, I was standing at the copy machine

when Jeff walked in. Not more than twenty-two years old and shivering, he carried a plastic grocery bag with a change of clothes and a Bible.

A Bible. Nice touch.

It was a Thursday and I hadn't even begun writing my sermon, so the last thing I needed was the distraction of an addict looking for a handout.

Trying to hide my irritation, I said, "Can I help you?"

"Yeah, uh . . . I was just released from jail a week ago and don't have anyplace to go," he said. "I need to talk to someone."

"Okay," I said. "But you need to know that we don't have food here."

That should do it. Sermon distraction averted.

"Well, food would have been nice, but I understand."

"And we don't give out money, either," I said. *Now leave. I have important things to write about Jesus and stuff.*

"That makes sense." He clutched his bag to his chest. "Are you the pastor?"

"Yes. I am."

"Would you mind if we talked?"

I hesitated for a moment. "Sure. Come on into my office. Want some coffee?"

You have ten minutes.

"Coffee would be great."

I learned that Jeff had grown up in a single-parent home in a very bad neighborhood and had spent the last two years in prison on drug charges. While Jeff was locked up, a man came to the prison every week to teach a Bible study. Through that study, Jeff became a Christian and began to learn about God's love for him in Christ. The man gave Jeff his own Bible, which he read cover to cover many times.

He had been looking for a job since he got out, but without a permanent residence or facilities to shave and shower, he found employers were unwilling to hire him.

"I'm not looking for a handout," he said, "but I am getting desperate and don't want to go back to the life I had before. I found a place to stay. It's only a hundred dollars a week, but the landlord requires two weeks up front. I also found a job in the kitchen of a pub, but I have to have an address first. I could walk to work from this apartment."

We talked for more than an hour. Finally, I said, "Come on. Let's go see this place."

So much for working on my sermon today.

The apartment was on the back side of an old house that had been divided into separate living units. Apart from the bathroom, it was a single room with a sink, a small refrigerator, and an ancient electric stove with only one working burner. A rusty bed sat in the corner, and there was a table and one chair across the room. The carpet had seen better days, but not recently, and the walls were in desperate need of paint. The place hadn't been cleaned in years, but it had potential.

We went to the grocery store and bought a couple weeks' worth of food, a razor and shaving cream, toothbrush, soap, and other essentials. Jeff was about my size so I brought him some old clothes and a jacket from home. He started work the next day.

The next few years were far from smooth sailing for Jeff.

He changed jobs often and occasionally got picked up for failing to report to his parole officer or for being out past his court-dictated curfew. He worshiped with us regularly and after a while nobody seemed to notice the teardrop tattoo on his cheek. He eventually began the process of getting approval to go back into the prison to lead a weekly Bible study. I wrote letters recommending him and giving him the sanction of teaching in the prison under the ministry of our church. He was only a couple of weeks away from approval when he missed yet another appointment with his parole officer. He would now have to serve the remainder of his original sentence, which amounted to more than two years.

With stoic optimism, Jeff wrote, "Well, Pastor, I guess I get to do prison ministry full-time now!"

Yes, Jeff, I guess you do.

THE TRUE FAST

As Christians, we do not have the freedom to blithely ignore the poor, homeless, and marginalized around us. Certainly, we need to be discerning, so long as that is not a justification for cold indifference. In fact, a posture of apathy toward those in need can have significant spiritual consequences for our own lives.

Isaiah 58 marks a time when the Israelites were going through their religious rituals and could not understand why God was not hearing their cries and answering their prayers. They said to God, "Why have we fasted . . . and you have not seen it? Why have we humbled ourselves, and you have not noticed?" (Isaiah 58:3).

God replied, "During your fast, you are cruel to your workers and quarrel amongst yourselves. Your fast is all a religious show. Do you think that's what I want from you?" (Isaiah 58:3-5, my paraphrase).

"The fast I want from you," said God, "is to loosen the bonds of oppression, share your food with the hungry, and give shelter to the homeless" (Isaiah 58:6-7, my paraphrase).

Our instincts are often just like those of the Israelites—to do more religious activities to try to get more of God in our lives. And we wonder why being religious hasn't really worked.

God says that when we reach into the pain of others—the briarpatch of their lives—and help to carry their burdens, it brings us closer to his heart. That doesn't mean we have to take on the mantle of solving world hunger or anything like that. It can be as simple as reaching out to the friendless and broken in our neighborhoods and communities, offering a listening ear and a caring heart. When we break the yoke of loneliness and alienation, God draws near.

I challenge you to reach beyond the four walls of your home or church and touch the lives of your neighbors, helping to remove their yokes of guilt, loneliness, poverty, or abuse. And see if you don't find yourself nearer to the heart of God. See if the Kingdom doesn't begin to come in your life and in the lives of others.

Then your light will break out like the dawn,
And your recovery will speedily spring forth;
And your righteousness will go before you;
The glory of the LORD will be your rear guard.

Then you will call, and the LORD will answer;
You will cry, and He will say, "Here I am."
If you remove the yoke from your midst,
The pointing of the finger and speaking wickedness,
And if you give yourself to the hungry
And satisfy the desire of the afflicted,
Then your light will rise in darkness
And your gloom will become like midday.

ISAIAH 58:8-10, NASB

God delights in his people when our hearts are synchronized with his heart, when our desires for our lives match up with his purposes for his Kingdom. When the hungry are fed, the poor are cared for, and justice established, God will be right in the thick of it and his people will be a light for the world. This is what Jesus meant when he taught us to pray, "Your kingdom come, your will be done, on earth as it is in heaven" (Matthew 6:10). Charity, equity, compassion, love, mercy—these are hallmarks of God's Kingdom, and he intends for them to be manifest here on earth.

In Luke 7:19, John the Baptist sends his followers to Jesus to ask, "Are you the one who is to come, or should we expect someone else?" In other words, "Are you the Messiah sent from God to change the world?"

Jesus answers, "Go back and report to John what you have seen and heard: The blind receive sight, the lame walk, those who have leprosy are cleansed, the deaf hear, the dead are raised, and the good news is proclaimed to the poor" (Luke 7:22). In other words, "When you see compassion, alleviation of suffering, love for others, care for the poor, you see God's Kingdom." It's not too much to say that we will not see God's Kingdom without these things. They are signs that Jesus has come and that his Kingdom is real. Compassion, healing, and love speak to the presence and reality of Jesus just as much today as they did when Jesus was on earth.

It's easy for Christians to assume that if we just get people in every nation to *believe* in Jesus, the consummation of God's Kingdom will arrive. That is, if we *tell* people about Jesus, we have accomplished our purpose. Well, proclamation of the truth is certainly important, but what about *demonstrating* the life that Jesus modeled? Is that not a more direct and effective way to see the Kingdom of God revealed on earth as it is in heaven?

The truth is, this is something we all can do. Most Christians fold up like a lawn chair at the thought of being "evangelistic." No way do we want to go to a mall, much less to our neighbors, and randomly start telling them all about Jesus. But what if we went just to be friends? What if we stood up for the poor single mom being shafted by her insurance company? What if we listened and cried with a classmate who just lost her father? Or helped the elderly couple next door patch their roof? Or brought a meal to the family whose son just went back into the hospital for further cancer treatment? What if we each met the needs of just *one* person who was hungry, lonely, or oppressed?

God says, "Your light will break forth like the dawn" (Isaiah 58:8). Isn't that the kind of Christian we all want to be? Isn't that the kind of Christian your neighbors, no matter their faith commitment, would want you to be? Isn't that the kind of person you can be? You may not be solving world hunger, but should that stop you from doing what you can?

What would it look like for you to care about just one person in your neighborhood? What if we all focused on just one person who is illiterate, an immigrant, a battered woman, or a fatherless child? We could begin to change our cities. At the very least, we would make a difference in that one life. "Your light will rise in the darkness, and your night will become like the noonday" (Isaiah 58:10). Do we believe that?

There were days when I didn't want to make Mr. Buford a sandwich, take him to the doctor, find him one of my old jackets, or give him an odd job so he could earn some money. I didn't even want to sit with him on the porch and talk. But I realize now that never in my life did the light of God's presence and pleasure shine as brightly as it did over those three years. It has been my experience that when we take the inconvenient path of entering into the life of one who is in need, we find God. It seems that's where he delights to be and where he bids us to join him, if we dare.

IN THE PATH OF THE STORM

"Enthusiastic" doesn't even begin to describe Ray Cannata. He sleeps about three hours a night, and that is simply the compromise his brain has worked out with his body. In the perpetual hyperdrive of his mind, nothing is immune to analysis. Whether it's the dangers of the pharmaceutical industry, the stupidity of standardized personality profiles, or how hot dogs represent a concerted government effort to undermine the moral freedom and fabric of our society, Ray has a theory. And it is usually a good one.

To know Ray Cannata is to enter a rabbit hole of brilliance and humor one never knew existed. Yet of all the people I am privileged to call my friends, none has embodied life in the briarpatch like Ray.

For fourteen years, Ray served as a pastor in one of the wealthiest counties per capita in the nation—and he was bored out of his skull. Hearing that a small congregation in the heart of New Orleans was looking for a pastor, he put in his name for consideration and waited to see how it would go.

As it turns out, Ray was asked to become the new pastor of the church in New Orleans and was invited down for a meeting on Monday, August 29, 2005.

He never made it to that meeting.

A tropical storm developing in the Gulf of Mexico had grown to become the hurricane we now know as Katrina, and it hit the coast shortly after six o'clock that morning.

Prior to Katrina, New Orleans was already a difficult place to live, much less serve as a pastor. It had the highest poverty and murder rates in the country, and its public schools ranked among the absolute worst. New Orleans was a city known for rampant political corruption, fiscal mismanagement, and a grossly decayed public works infrastructure. The potholes in New Orleans were known to swallow entire cars and seemed to have a personality of their own.

And that was before Katrina.

The storm flooded 80 percent of the city's homes, schools, and businesses, and killed one out of every three hundred residents. It caused $80 billion in damages and brought tourism to a standstill. The tax base of this already struggling city was wiped out overnight.

Many homes did not qualify for flood insurance and their owners waited in vain for promised funds from FEMA. Eighteen months after the storm, 61,000 families would still be living in temporary trailers no bigger than many suburban kitchens.

The church that had called Ray to be their new pastor reflected the devastation of the city. Two-thirds of the small congregation left the city permanently after the storm, leaving only seventeen members. For all intents and purposes, the church was gone.

Nobody would have blamed Ray for declining the offer to go to New Orleans and deciding to remain securely ensconced in his comfortable pastorate in the suburbs of New York City. But that was not Ray. Where others saw a dead end, Ray saw an opportunity to follow Jesus into the briarpatch—and that's what he did.

Once the water receded, Ray and his wife, Kathy, packed up their belongings, loaded their two small children in the car, and made their way south to a city and a church that had been reduced to rubble. Instead of shying away from trouble, Ray brought all of his brilliance and passion to bear upon this devastated city, and the results were nothing short of astonishing.

After the water receded, the church opened its doors again.

Thirty-five people were in attendance on Ray's first Sunday, and all had been broken and battered by the storm. They were certainly bewildered, confused, and concerned for themselves and for their neighbors. Ray recalls those first days: "Everybody thought we needed an Oprah moment—a big hug, with everybody feeling everybody's pain. I said no; what we needed was to serve our community. We didn't need coddling; we needed a mission." Ray knew what it would take for the light of God to shine in the soggy darkness of New Orleans. He had an idea, and it eventually changed the lives of thousands.

To get things rolling, he used $1000 of the church's funds to purchase construction tools and supplies. He and his congregation set to work on repairing a home that Ray envisioned would serve as a base for volunteers who would come to New Orleans from around the country to repair damaged homes. For the next few years, thousands came, year-round, to help with the rebuilding and restoration.

With boundless energy and essentially no money, Ray and his congregation recruited and coordinated teams of volunteers, pairing them with homeowners who had nowhere else to turn. Hope slowly began to return to New Orleans as homes were rebuilt one at a time and the temporary trailers were hauled away. As I write this in the spring of 2012, almost seven years after Katrina, Ray and his congregation have assisted in rebuilding nearly five hundred homes. And they're still going.

If you were to ask Ray why he moved to New Orleans in the face of such long odds and immeasurable suffering, he would tell you that it's because he believes the gospel of Jesus is true and that it calls us to move toward the pain and suffering of the world. As Christians, we do not have the luxury of sitting back and doing nothing while fellow human beings suffer. We go where the need is greatest—we move toward the suffering.

And so he went.

There was never any illusion in Ray's overactive mind that he could solve even a fraction of the problems caused by Katrina, but that didn't stop him. After being in New Orleans for a year, he wrote, "I can't get past the firm conclusion that the Spirit of God is moving in stunning ways across our city. It is amazing [to see] what is happening in hearts, if my tiny slice of the big story here is anything."[1]

He knew he couldn't save them all, so he worked on saving one at a time. Believe me when I tell you that if Ray and his tiny congregation can do it, so can you. And it doesn't have to be on such a large scale. It may be only a coworker struggling with addiction who needs encouragement, or a neighbor who is going through a divorce and needs nothing more than an open heart and a listening ear. You can make the difference in someone's life, if you dare to enter the briarpatch.

A FAMILY BIRTHDAY

We had just finished dinner one evening several years ago when Mr. Buford stopped by to visit. It was a cold night and his joints were stiff and aching. "Used to be cold didn't bother me, but now it do. Reckon I'm gettin' old."

Carrie brought him a warm plate of baked chicken and vegetables and a glass of sweet tea. He always loved her cooking and was never shy about letting her know.

I said, "You're not old, Mr. Buford. I think you could still take me."

"I am gettin' old. Know how I know? Today's my birthday."

"Ha! We had no idea! Well, happy birthday!" I said.

"Yeah," he said, "I'm sixty-four years old today."

I raised my glass and offered a toast to our friend, Mr. Buford, "May God give us many more years together."

We talked for quite some time. Mr. Buford entertained us with more stories from his life. He told us how the abandoned house next to ours used to be a crack house until the police came and cleared it out. He talked about his wife and how he wished they'd had kids. But mostly he talked about God, and how blessed he was to be here, on this night, with us.

Our youngest daughter, who was about six at the time, came out with a gift for Mr. Buford. It was a homemade card of construction paper decorated with crayon drawings. There were stick figures of each of our family members and one of Mr. Buford, too, right in the middle of us all. It read, "Happy Birthday, Mr. Buford."

CHAPTER 9

MISSING PIECES
FINDING THE MEANING OF JESUS IN THE CRUCIBLE OF SUFFERING

Now it seems to me that love of some
kind is the only possible explanation of the
extraordinary amount of suffering that there
is in the world.

OSCAR WILDE

You must submit to supreme suffering in order
to discover the completion of joy.

JOHN CALVIN

Fairy tales are more than true; not because
they tell us that dragons exist, but because
they tell us that dragons can be beaten.

G. K. CHESTERTON

His face was ashen, his voice awkward. As an orthopedist, he wasn't supposed to have to deal with this, especially with people he had just met.

But I pressed, "What are you saying?"

His shoulders sagged as he spoke in a languid, broken whisper. "She has cancer."

Carrie and I were terrified. "She" was Emma, our five-

159

year-old daughter. In a split second, someone had pulled the emergency brake of the freight train that had been our life thus far. Loaded with a cargo of hopes, dreams, and best-laid plans, we were speeding along unencumbered and optimistic about what lay ahead. Now, crushed against the bulkhead, all my aspirations for Emma's future and our family shattered and splintered about me. I labored to breathe.

Bewildered and choking on the rising panic, I had no idea that what I would soon come to learn about God would change me forever.

About five months earlier, Emma had started kindergarten. Dropping her off each morning on my way to the office, we were greeted in the carpool line by her kind and cheerful teacher. After getting my good-bye kiss from Emma, I would watch her bouncing pigtails as she skipped into the building.

One day, Emma began complaining that her back hurt. This was a pain I knew all too well, but it was odd for a five-year-old. She had recently fallen at recess, so Carrie and I didn't think much of it, giving her children's Tylenol and telling her it would feel better in a day or two. When the pain persisted into the next week, we took her to have her back X-rayed. Everything looked fine, but the pain remained for months with no explanation, until the morning of February 11, 2003.

We awoke in the middle of the night to Emma's screaming in pain and vomiting in her bed. All she could manage was a shrill, "My back hurts!"

Having my own experience with back injuries, we got her stabilized flat on the floor with her legs elevated on a pillow to relieve the pressure. After two hours, Emma stopped crying and fell asleep. We knew we needed to take her to the doctor, but she shrieked in agony whenever we tried to move her. We decided to wait until morning.

We had no idea she could no longer move her legs.

The next morning, we took our son to school and got a friend to watch our toddler while we made the drive to Scottish Rite Children's Hospital in Atlanta for another X-ray. Our family doctor told us that this would be the best place to start. Had I known what it was we were "starting," I would not have been able to take that first step.

The X-ray went smoothly. I gingerly carried Emma to the room and laid her softly on the table. Two quick pictures and we were back in the exam room.

The doctor said, "It should only take a few minutes to get the film back." He walked out of the room and left the door about five inches ajar.

Not long after, a scrub-clad figure slid the film into an acrylic file holder attached to the door. I thought, *Wow, that was fast. I should be back at the office by noon.* The first sign of impending bad news came when the doctor removed the film, glanced at it again as he turned to push the exam room door open, and then stopped. I mean he stopped *dead* in his tracks and stared at the image in his hands, disbelief on his face. I don't think he knew I could see him.

The second sign came when he turned, film in hand, and *ran* down the hall. I've watched enough TV medical dramas to know that doctors *don't* run. Unless, that is, something is terribly wrong. And it was.

He eventually came back to our examining room. "Sorry. I had to consult with my colleagues."

Sign number three.

"Let me show you something."

He slid the X-ray from five months prior onto the lightbox attached to the wall. "This is your daughter's spine. This is how we want it to look."

"Now look at this." He put up the new X-ray. I didn't have to be an MD to see that the two appeared very different.

"Her vertebrae from here to here," he said as he pointed to the ghostly image, "have shattered and compressed on one another." They looked like marshmallows that someone had squeezed between their thumb and forefinger. Then, without taking a breath he continued, "I'm sending you over to the ER. I've called ahead and they are expecting you. A hematologist will be waiting for you."

There was a note of panic in his voice that I had never heard from a doctor. It sent chills down my own, fully intact, spine.

"Wait a minute," I said as I tried to gather myself. "What are you saying?"

"They will fill you in when they see you over at the ER."

"No." Locking eyes, I made it clear I was not leaving without more information. "Our daughter's spine is crushed, seemingly all on its own, and now you are sending us to see a *blood* doctor? What are you not telling us?"

He hesitated, glancing at my wife and then at my daughter. Turning away from Emma, he whispered, "I can't confirm this. They will have to do some tests, but I think your daughter has leukemia."

"You *think*?" But from his pallid face I knew he wasn't just guessing.

His whisper had concussive force. "She has cancer."

MISSING PIECES

Everyone experiences suffering on some level. The truth is, bad stuff happens irrespective of age, race, social or economic status, religion, or political affiliation. It does not matter if we live in the suburbs or the city, work in the White House or at the Waffle House. Suffering is a universal problem for all of humanity. Even if it's not our daughter who has cancer, our spouse who was killed in a car accident, or our brother who overdosed, we can't help but be touched by the tragic presence of suffering through our friends, neighbors, classmates, and coworkers. Suffering is everywhere, and we know instinctively that it is evil and we are repulsed by its presence in our world. It isn't supposed to happen.

My brother-in-law's Humvee was not supposed to get blown up in Iraq, leading to countless reconstructive surgeries and forever maiming him inside and out. But it did. If you have ever been with someone when they received the horrific news of the death of a loved one, you have heard the chilling, ethereal moan of the soul as a heart is wrenched in two. I have caught people in my arms as they absorb the bad news. I have melted with them to the floor, their uncontrolled wailing shattering my insides, and I will never be reconciled to the unwelcomed invasion of death and evil in our world. Thankfully, because the gospel of Jesus Christ is true, I don't have to be. Still, my good friend's wife was not supposed to die of a brain tumor while in the prime of her life. But she did.

Why?

To be honest, I have been sitting here staring at the blinking cursor and I don't have the answer, at least not one that can bring clarity and closure. Sure, there are many possible responses, but trying to figure out why God allows suffering in the world he has made is a bit like putting together a jigsaw puzzle without having all the pieces. Suffering and the very real presence of evil pose a problem for us all, but that does not stop us from seeking answers, no matter what our position of faith.

In polytheistic worldviews, the answer to suffering arises out of the idea that there is some combination of good gods and bad gods. One is not necessarily more powerful than the others. Neither is one smarter, more cunning, or more present. But there's a big, cosmic skirmish going on, and from time to time we become the collateral damage of their celestial bickering. Sure, we can root for the good guys, but other than that, there is nothing really to get all worked up about. Evil happens because the gods sometimes behave badly. That's one explanation.

For many people, that just doesn't hold water. The problem of the continuance of suffering in our lives and throughout the world leads some to believe there is no God at all. Evil is just the way the world is sometimes. In short, the explanation is that there *is* no explanation. But that doesn't solve anything. Rather, it creates even more difficulty and makes suffering and evil more problematic.

The temptation to jettison God in the midst of horrific

tragedy and unbearable pain is understandable. I know because I have been there. But getting rid of God doesn't make the problem of evil and suffering any easier to handle. In fact, it robs us of *any* answer or explanation.

If there is not a supreme, divine being of some sort, who is by definition good and just, then it seems to me we have no basis on which to say that evil is actually evil or that anything is actually bad or ought not to happen.

Jean-Paul Sartre, no friend of Christianity, says it well:

> The existentialist . . . finds it extremely embarrassing that God does not exist, for there disappears with Him all possibility of finding values in an intelligible heaven. There can no longer be any good *a priori*, since there is no infinite and perfect consciousness to think it. It is nowhere written that "the good" exists, that one must be honest or not lie, since we are now upon the plane where there are only men. Dostoevsky once wrote, "If God did not exist, everything would be permitted"; and that, for existentialism, is the starting point. Everything is indeed permitted if God does not exist, and man is in consequence forlorn, for he cannot find anything to depend upon either within or outside himself.[1]

In other words, somebody has to say, "This is good and that is bad. This is right and that is wrong. This is the way it should be and that is out of place." There has to be an objective standard that transcends subjective human opinion and experience. Otherwise, our pain and suffering are diluted in a wash of relativity.

Without God and his standard of what is good and right, we might *feel* that the suffering we experience is wrong; but it would just be a feeling because when we remove God, we have no basis on which to say that death, violence, suffering, injustice, or any other malady is anything more than "just the way it is." Can you really imagine saying to someone who is dealing with tragedy, "Hey, stuff happens"? If you had said that to me at the time of Emma's cancer diagnosis, it would have taken a team of oncologists (and then some) to peel me off of you, and I believe I would have had Jesus on my side in the fray.

WHY DOES GOD ALLOW EVIL AND SUFFERING?

If the answer to evil and suffering is not "gods gone wild" or "God has left the building," then what is it? You might assume I'm going to say that Christianity has the answer. Well, yes—and no. I'm convinced that belief in the reality of God is the only way to even begin dealing effectively with suffering and evil. And I believe God *has* answered the problem of evil and suffering, but he hasn't given us all the answers, or even all the big answers.

But even though we may not have all the answers or all the pieces of the puzzle, it doesn't mean that we, as Christians, have nothing to say. Let's start with what we *do* know.

The Bible teaches, and Christians believe, there is a God. One God. The true and living God, who is all-loving and absolutely powerful. He is not an emotionally absent deity who arbitrarily made the world on a day when he didn't have anything better to do, and then suddenly got bored with it all and left it to fend for itself, collecting dust on a shelf in his cosmic workshop. The Bible is replete with examples of God's intervention in the affairs of this world, in ways that demonstrate his care and compassion for what he has made and his concern for what happens here—culminating in the sacrifice of his own Son on our behalf. With that one act alone, he established himself as a God who loves on a scale we can scarcely imagine. That's why it simply won't do to say that the world is going to hell in a handbasket and God doesn't care, or that he must think it's not his problem. Love defines the essence of who God is. Whatever the answer might be to why he allows evil and suffering, it can't be that he doesn't care.

Not only is God all-loving, he is also all-powerful, as in create-the-world-out-of-nothing powerful. Theologians call this quality *omnipotence*. That's just a fancy way of saying that God can do whatever he wants, whenever he wants, for as long as he wants. He doesn't suddenly feel the need for a nap, only to have evil run amok while he drools and snores on the sofa. God cannot be worn out, and he cannot be overcome. He is not engaged in a cosmic arm-wrestling match with an equal (or even lesser) god, while the fate of the world hangs in the balance. Sure, evil is real and patently destructive in our lives, but it is not divine or even godlike, and it is not a threat to God. There's no stopping God.

So the answer can't be that evil has somehow gotten the

upper hand on God and now he is impotent to do anything about it or needs to regroup to devise another strategy.

God is good *and* mighty. This is what the Bible teaches, and it makes sense to me. But the Bible also teaches that suffering and evil are a terrible reality in our world. They are not figments of our imagination. Evil is a punch-you-in-the-face actuality that inflicts untold damage on our physical, emotional, spiritual, and relational existence. This is why Pollyannaish religious platitudes that look for the silver lining in every tragedy strike us as unsatisfying and leave us starving for more meaningful answers. To say to a couple who just lost their unborn child, "God works all things together for the good for those who love him," is abusive and a cop-out. It is a denial of their palpable, present suffering and does no good.

But saying—even *knowing*—that God is all-loving and all-powerful still does not seem to answer the question of why he allows evil and suffering. If there's no stopping God, what's stopping him? The truth is, I have never found an adequate answer to that question. Still, I choose to trust—based on what I *do* know about God—that his purpose is ultimately good and redemptive, even if it is painful and confusing.

So as we venture into the briarpatch, what can we say? What hope do we have? Is there an answer? Yes, there is. And it speaks directly to the brokenness that has shattered the world we live in.

WE ARE NOT BUILT FOR THIS

Emma was in chemotherapy over the course of two years. During that time, we were constantly in and out of the hospital. We always had a bag packed, and on many occasions we had to rush to the hospital in the middle of the night. This introduced an extraordinary amount of uncertainty into our schedule and family routine. For that reason, one or the other of Emma's grandmothers was always living with us, ready to care for the other kids while Carrie and I spent days on end with our daughter in a twelve-by-eighteen-foot room stuffed with monitors and hanging IV bags.

Because someone was always flying in or out, I made a lot of trips to the airport. On one such drive, I flipped through the radio stations for something to fill the silence. Since Emma's diagnosis, much of what was considered popular music struck me as part of an optimistic fantasy world that had become foreign to me. Mine was a world of unanswerable questions, crushing despair, and uncertainty. Every song I heard was a ballad of banality that conjured up cynicism and anger from the dark crevasse that had split me open inside.

After exhausting the FM dial with no success, I switched over to the AM side to see what brilliance was under discussion on talk radio. Sports . . . *nope*. Car repair . . . *I don't think so*. Gardening . . . *not today*. Politics . . . *like I need more misery and cynicism in my life!*

As I pushed the scan button one more time, I heard a radio host ask his guest, "So what did you do when you heard the news?"

The guest's response provided me an exit ramp from my interminable road of emotional, intellectual, and theological despair.

His young teenage daughter had gotten pregnant, and he

and his wife were trying to decide the best way to navigate the difficult and confusing terrain before them. He said, "Well, I was lost. But eventually I realized there's not a good way of going through something like this—because, as a human being, I was not built for this. This is not the way God intended for things to be."

In many ways, that was the major piece that was missing from my puzzle of bewilderment and doubt.

"This is not the way God intended for things to be."

I had read many books, chapters, essays, and articles on suffering, sickness, and dealing with tragedy. Many were sent from all over the world by friends and family who wanted to offer comfort and hope. Though I read them all, I was generally left feeling that the authors didn't really understand what I was going through.

They all said the same things and quoted the Bible a lot. But I have a theology degree and had read the Bible cover-to-cover again and again. I already knew that God loved me and that he provides for the sparrow and the lilies of the field. I knew Jesus wept over the death of his friend Lazarus. I knew that God wins in the end.

I didn't need to be reminded of all this. I knew most of these things by heart and still believed them firmly. I never doubted God's affection for me. But I also knew that my kid had cancer and was dying. And I felt so gravely alone and could not figure out how I was supposed to walk this road.

And then some guy on the radio provided the missing piece: "There's not a good way of going through something like this—because, as a human being, I was not built for this."

For the first time since this nightmare had begun, I felt as if there was someone else who believed in God and understood where I was. He understood my desperate search for a good way to navigate what I thought was my godforsaken journey, for finding answers in this parched and desolate land.

Just hearing that there is no *good* path was water to my desiccated soul.

God did not build me or you or anyone else for something like this, because he never intended for us to have to deal with such destruction and agony. This is not the way his world was, or is, supposed to function. Cancer in children is a foreign invader with which we can never be reconciled as members of God's good creation. It would be like getting a handful of sand in your eyes and saying, "It's okay, I'll figure out a way to deal with the excruciating pain!" That makes no sense. The sand is not supposed to be there, and nothing will be as it is supposed to be until you get it out. I am no more built for watching my five-year-old battle leukemia than my eyes are designed to be a repository for finely granulated rock and mineral particles.

Suddenly, I had something more than, "Hold on! Jesus wins in the end!" to comfort me. As true as that is, it brings scant consolation and seems to minimize the acute struggle of the moment. Is God *only* concerned about how it all works out in the end? In the meantime, is our best hope to pull ourselves up by the bootstraps and stop all our whining? Absolutely not! The reason God did not build us for this is because he never intended for it to be a part of our lives in the first place. In other words, he is not merely concerned that we have eternal life someday, but that we live the life of eternity—his life—today.

I realized this is why Jesus came into this world that is often an unfair briarpatch of broken hearts and fractured dreams. He came not just so that you and I can go to heaven one day but because this world he created is broken and needs to be fixed. Cancer, hunger, slavery, injustice, oppression, betrayal, violence, racism, classism, and a thousand other destructive infections need to be cured. Jesus came because my daughter is not supposed to get cancer. His incarnation and death and resurrection hit the pavement on my street, where I live, like it never had before. I knew it might not mean that my daughter would survive, but it did mean that my deep sadness was valid. Even more, it was understood and I was not alone.

I know this is not something I can prove, but I knew then that Jesus was weeping along with me. He feels the same rage toward evil and suffering that I feel (John 11:33). Is it possible that my anger and hatred of the brokenness of the world is justified? I think it is more than justified. It's biblical. And so is yours.

When Jesus came, he didn't tiptoe around the turmoil and struggle of humanity; he jumped headlong into it. He was called the "man of sorrows" for a reason. He was familiar with suffering (see Isaiah 53:3, KJV). In fact, we read in Hebrews 5:7-9, "During the days of Jesus' life on earth, he offered up prayers and petitions with fervent cries and tears to the one who could save him from death, and he was heard because of his reverent submission. Son though he was, he learned obedience from what he suffered and, once made perfect, he became the source of eternal salvation for all who obey him." His being familiar with suffering was somehow essential to his identity as our Savior. When he came, he came into the briarpatch.

When we experience the effects of tragedy and brokenness and ask God, "Why do you allow this?" we don't really know the reason. But we do know what the reason *is not*. It can't be that God is remote or indifferent, because he already came and immersed himself among the thistles and barbs of human suffering. And he didn't do it because he's a glutton for punishment or an adrenaline junkie. He did it to identify with us in every way.

Likewise, it can't be because he doesn't care. It was out of his love for the world that Jesus came in the first place. And it can't be because he lacks the power to do anything about it. The Cross of Jesus was *precisely* the act of God that will ultimately defeat evil and restore the world to God's order and purpose. Colossians 1:19-20 says, "For God was pleased to have all his fullness dwell in him, and through him to reconcile to himself all things, whether things on earth or things in heaven, by making peace through his blood, shed on the cross."

EMPATHY AMID THE THORNS

I was at our local pub having lunch with a friend, when David, one of the owners, slid into the booth next to me. I had gotten to know David over the past three years, and when Emma was diagnosed, he showed great concern and compassion for my family and me. He doesn't go to church or anything, but my being a pastor didn't seem to be of particular concern to him.

He always greeted me with a hearty handshake or hug and asked, "How's she doing?"

"Hey," he said, "knowing what you are going through, I was wondering if you could go over and talk to another friend of mine. His teenage son was just diagnosed with a brain tumor."

As a pastor, I had been asked to do such things many times before and had never felt that it went particularly well. I would, for example, tap nervously on the door to the hospital room, apologetically enter, and be terrified they would ask a question I didn't know the answer to, or start lashing out at God and by proxy lash out at me. In the best scenarios, they would smile and I would set the flowers or balloons on the table by the mirror. I would sit down next to the bed while we proceeded to ignore the terror in the room. I would ask politely about the latest news from the doctor and they would be just as polite in keeping their answers on the surface. After reading a short passage from the Bible and praying for them, I would leave.

Whether in the hospital or in their homes, that's pretty much how it would go every time. I always felt like a failure. Not knowing that this time would be any different, I walked over to the bar and slid onto the stool next to Victor, held out my hand, and said, "Hi, I'm Shayne. David tells me you are dealing with some pretty rough stuff. I have a kid with cancer too. Mind if I join you?"

He said, "Sure," so I ordered something to drink.

"Tell me about your son," I said. "What's he like?"

Most often, when you or someone you love is struck by

disease or tragedy of any kind, they easily become defined by that tragedy. They become "the kid with cancer" or "the guy with a meth addiction" or "the woman whose husband was hit by a drunk driver." It begins to feel as if they've lost their identity in the eyes of the watching world, like they are no longer the person who loves dogs or sci-fi movies or gardening or their work at the CDC.

"He's a skateboarder," Victor said. "Really good, in fact. He wears all the grungy clothes and his hair is a mess. But he's a good kid; our oldest."

He talked on for a bit. I listened and imagined the great kid he was describing, allowing my heart to begin to break.

"Tell me about your other kids. You married?"

He talked more and seemed to be happy to talk about something other than cancer.

Eventually, I asked, "So when was he diagnosed?"

"A few days ago."

Silence. We both sipped our drinks. I had no solutions, at least none that he really wanted to hear at that moment. I did, however, have one of the most powerfully healing things that human beings have to offer one another in times of crisis: *sympathy*. Actually, in this case, it was empathy because I had been there in my own life.

"It stinks, doesn't it?" I said.

"Yeah, it's like everything has changed," he admitted. "We're scared and don't know what to do." He spoke more about the last few days, their confusion and disillusionment, their abject terror and pain, not knowing how to get through the day, much less the next week or month or year.

After a while I said, "I am really sorry this has happened, Victor. And I don't know whether or not you care what God thinks about this, or if you even believe in God. But I believe in God and can tell you that he thinks this stinks too. He is weeping alongside you. Our kids are not supposed to get cancer. That's not how he set it all up."

"Yeah, but my kid *did* get cancer."

After another brief silence, I said, "You know, Christians talk a lot about Jesus dying for our sins, and I agree with that. I believe that. But I think there's more to it. He didn't die just so you or I can go to heaven one day; he died for all the non-spiritual stuff, too, like disease, addiction, hunger, and abuse. I don't have to tell you that those things are out of place in our world. And they are just as much a part of the reason why God sent Jesus. Jesus came not just because people are screwed up and need God; he came because the whole world is off balance. This doesn't mean we have any guarantees about our kids, but it does mean that it hasn't escaped God's attention and you are not alone. He is going to put the world to rights. I just wish he would hurry up about it."

Victor's son died a few weeks later. Our church now supports an annual fund-raiser for cancer research in his memory. It's called SkaterAid. The parking lot we share with other businesses is transformed into a huge skate park complete with two stages for bands to play. Art created and donated for sale hangs throughout our lobby. A lot of money is raised each year. Raising money won't bring Victor's son back or even assuage the pain of his death, but it is a communal acknowledgment that cancer is an enemy that needs to be defeated.

Emma survived her bout with leukemia and is now a thriving teenager. There are some lingering complications, but her vertebrae healed and she regained feeling in her legs and her ability to walk. She only just recently became more comfortable talking about her battle. I think the experience was just more than her young heart could process. She made friends during her many stays on the pediatric oncology floor. She lost some of them too. Some of her closest friends today are kids who had, or have, cancer. I guess she will always be a part of that club. Some of them have relapsed. Death is never far away from her world, and that is a horrible briarpatch of extreme proportions. But we know that God is never far away either. He is here, in this briarpatch with her, and with you. I am here, too, as are many of my friends and your friends.

It's not as scary as you might think to enter into the confused and broken lives of those dealing with tragedy. Leave the platitudes at home and just bring yourself.

CHAPTER 10

LOOKING FOR
THE RAINBOW
DOES GOD REALLY
HATE GAYS?

A Christian is supposed to care about
a just society for *all* our neighbors,
whether they believe like we do or not.
And that's gotta mean our gay neighbor.
TIMOTHY KELLER

What is straight? A line can be straight,
or a street, but the human heart, oh,
no, it's curved like a road through
mountains.
TENNESSEE WILLIAMS,
A STREETCAR NAMED DESIRE

During the Alexandrian plague in the mid-third century,
Christians risked their lives in caring for the sick, taking a
posture of grace that said, "I am here for you. I may die, but
you will not be alone." The church embodied the gospel, and
the message was not forgotten.

In the 1980s, when the AIDS epidemic hit the gay community, the church again had an opportunity to care for the
sick and speak grace to the afflicted. This time, however,
instead of showing compassion, many Christians spewed

venom, self-righteously proclaiming God's judgment. The message came through loud and clear.

And it has not been forgotten.

When Greg, who is gay, discovered I was a pastor, his demeanor changed and he lit into me with a pain-filled—and painful—diatribe. His wounds had a history and it all came out. After a few minutes of his hyperbolic invective, I stopped him with these words: "Tell you what, if you don't assume I'm a gay-hating bigot, I won't assume you're a pedophile. Deal? If we buy into stereotypes, we'll never be able to love one another."

Tears streamed down his face as he said, "Are you *sure* you're a Christian?"

Now I had tears of my own.

Christians may say, "Love the sinner; hate the sin," but what Greg and many other homosexuals hear is, "God hates fags" because that is the slogan they too often see written on the poster boards at rallies and protests. It's shameful. It's wrong. And it's our fault.

It may look different from one person to the next, but sin has fractured *every* human soul (Romans 3:23; 5:12; 1 John 1:10). As Aleksandr Solzhenitsyn said, "The line dividing good and evil cuts through the heart of *every* human being."[1] It's high time we lived and loved as if we really believed that.

At our church, we regularly say, "As Christians, none of us has the freedom to live however we want. Man or woman, young or old, gay or straight—we are all under God's authority and called to conform our lives to Christ."

The Bible is clear: Homosexual practice is inconsistent with Christian discipleship. But there is not a special judgment reserved for homosexuals, nor is there a special righteousness set apart for heterosexuals. For all of us, our only hope for the fracture in our souls is the cross of Jesus Christ.[2]

WELCOME TO THE NEIGHBORHOOD, CHER

It was late summer when James and Ryan moved in two doors down. I had seen the moving truck and boxes and went over to introduce myself. One worked for a Fortune 500 company based in Atlanta; the other was a real estate agent. They had been together for a number of years and shared custody of Ryan's daughter with his ex-wife. Other than being gay, they were no different from any family in your neighborhood. They were delightful, funny, and generous.

About two weeks before we opened the doors of All Souls Fellowship for the first time, I went over to invite James and Ryan to join us on the first Sunday.

I rang the bell, unprepared for the spectacle.

The door swung open with a flourish and I was greeted with an enthusiastic "Haaaayy!" There was James in a loose, white tank top that went to just above his knees. On the shirt was a full-length, larger-than-life picture of Cher, in all her flamboyant glory. I stood there and let the moment sink in.

"Wow," I mocked playfully, "that's quite a shirt."

"I know! But isn't she fabulous?"

I knew at that moment this was going to be a wonderful friendship.

"Listen, I am a pastor and we are starting a new church here in Decatur a week from this Sunday. Here is a little information. I hope you and Ryan can come."

As James looked over the card, he said, "Good luck getting Ryan to come. He's not a Christian and will probably sleep in and then sit around smoking those stupid cigarettes. But I have been praying that God would provide a church for me here. I will definitely be there."

"Great."

"Can I wear my Cher shirt?" he asked.

"Dude, you can wear whatever you're most comfortable in."

James was there that first Sunday, smartly dressed in business casual.

A LOVER'S QUARREL

When we first moved to Decatur, it boasted the highest per capita gay and lesbian population in the country. In our neighborhood, a full one-third of the homes were gay or lesbian couples, and that was somewhat typical for the entire city. It was, and is, a culturally eclectic and endlessly interesting place to live. The human multiformity, I found, applied within the gay community as well.

The assumption that you can lump all gays and lesbians together—that there's some sort of standardized form— is patently untrue. I can assure you that not every lesbian loves Melissa Etheridge, plays softball, and owns stock in The Home Depot. Nor does every gay man have impeccable fashion sense, an overbearing mother, and a life scheduled around the Tony Awards. Being gay does not make someone a homogenous, one-dimensional being whose entire identity is centered on his or her sexual orientation.

Among my gay friends are singles and couples, men and

women, wealthy and middle-class, some with children, and some without. All with unique dreams and stories, but sharing a common wound. They all have experienced the rejection of Christians and have (rightly?) come to the conclusion that they are not welcome in the vast majority of churches. It seems we have conveyed the idea that the grace of Jesus, which covers the needs of a broken humanity, somehow does not apply to the openly gay lifestyle. The gay and lesbian community has received our snubbing missive loud and clear: There is no place for you here unless you change. There is a seemingly impenetrable barrier between the gay community and the church.

And it's not just gay folks who have understood our words and actions in this way. Our dismissive memo has been broadly circulated. According to David Kinnaman and Gabe Lyons in their book *UnChristian*, 91 percent of Mosaics and Busters (those born after 1964) who are outside the church view the church as "antihomosexual"—not just opposed to a gay lifestyle, but opposed to gay *people*. The way many churches, particularly in the evangelical tradition, have handled this issue has caused us to lose our voice with the vast majority of our friends and neighbors. Kinnaman and Lyons remark, "When you introduce yourself as a Christian to a friend, neighbor, or business associate who is an outsider, you might as well have it tattooed on your arm: antihomosexual, gay-hater, homophobic. I doubt you think of yourself in these terms, but that's what outsiders think of you."[3]

Emily Saliers, one-half of the Indigo Girls and a Decatur resident, was raised in the church and is the daughter of a pastor. Her description of her relationship with the church as a "lover's quarrel" is both beautiful and tragic. She is not unlike my gay and lesbian friends, many of whom have a deep sense of their need for God and an earnest affection for Jesus Christ, but have found themselves outside the community of faith looking in—in part because of our clumsy treatment of this confusing issue. Yet many of them are still pursuing Jesus in spite of ill treatment by the church. The majority of gay folks identify themselves as Christian, with one-third attending church regularly and one out of six holding "born again" beliefs.[4]

CHAMELEONS AND OXEN

Though not addressing the issue specifically, Dick Keyes, in his book *Chameleon Christianity*, gets at what I think is the heart of the problem between the church and the gay and lesbian community. He says the church has historically navigated to opposite ends of the spectrum in responding to difficult social and cultural issues. At one end, some have developed the characteristics of chameleons, blending seamlessly with their surroundings so as to become indistinguishable. These Christians have abdicated the uniqueness of Christ and anything that may be viewed by the culture as intolerant. What is left is a church that is quite indistinguishable from the secular culture—a church that has forfeited its redemptive voice. It is salt that has lost its saltiness.

On the other end are the "musk oxen." The musk ox, a large arctic animal that travels in herds, resembles a bison with curvy horns. When threatened, the herd forms a large circle, with horns facing outward. This is their means of defending

themselves against perceived threats. Much of evangelicalism
has postured itself in this fashion—defensive toward the men-
acing culture. Congregations have retreated into their own
little tribes, with their own sets of extrabiblical rules, rather
than actively engaging the culture with the good news of Jesus
Christ.[5]

I think Dick Keyes is dead on. We have chosen either to
blend in or bully, acquiesce or attack, and it has only led to
further polarization of God's people. But are we stuck with
only two choices—squishy syncretism or adversarial funda-
mentalism? I believe there's a third way, but it's a road less
traveled by the Christian church. It is full of uncertainty and
can be a frightening path for those who both take the Bible
seriously and seek to be faithful to Christ's calling to love our
neighbors—all of our neighbors.

In August 2009, I received an e-mail from a woman who
had visited our church with her partner and their daughter. I
get many e-mails like this. This family had a very positive experience, but had obvious questions. Here is part of her e-mail:

> [My partner] and I both were raised in the church
> and have remained committed to our relationship
> with Jesus Christ. We do, however, understand that
> some denominations and/or specific churches do
> not accept our lifestyle. We feel it is necessary to join
> a congregation that accepts and loves us for who
> we are, especially now that we have a child. We are
> wondering if All Souls is that type of congregation.
> I hope you are comfortable enough to answer my

question candidly, without fear of hard feelings on
our part. We completely respect the rights of people
to have differences of opinion, especially when it
comes to biblical interpretations. Frankly, we just
want to find a church home where we can raise a
family, volunteer, fellowship, and be stewards for
Christ, all while being accepted.

I hope you appreciate the kind and gentle tone of her words.
This woman, who has been speared by the horns of the
musk ox, maintains a posture of grace and understanding,
even though she has reason not to. Below is a portion of my
rather lengthy response. It shows the messiness of living in the
briarpatch.

Thanks for the question.
As a gay Christian, you already know there is
no easy answer. In our church, we try to walk that
fine line on which we can balance fidelity to the
Scripture, our command to love one another, and
what the gospel says about acceptance in Christ.
Often, our efforts to do this end up frustrating
many on both sides, but we think it is important to
be honest about what the Bible does, and does not,
say about our gay brothers and sisters. . . .
The honest truth is that this issue is a very, very
difficult one for the church. In my opinion, much
damage has been done by those on the conservative
side, who have essentially said that all practicing gay

folks are going to hell. That is not true. It is a denial
of the gospel. It has hurt a lot of people and, I think,
brought dishonor on the name of Christ.

Yet on the other side, it feels like others have
either ignored or tried to explain away what the
Bible does say. I do not assume ill intent on the part
of these brothers and sisters and I think I understand
why they do this. In all honesty, I am sure I do the
very same thing with the parts of Scripture I don't
like!!! But when we stray from God's self-revelation
in the Scripture, we are in danger of creating God in
our own image, which makes him a false god. It is
something we all must be careful to avoid.

So all of this to say we are willing to walk into
the tension. Historically, the church has not done
this well, and we truly want to have the courage to
walk down some uncharted paths. I am sure we have
at times erred on both sides in our efforts to both
respect our gay brothers and sisters in Christ and
be honest about what we believe the Bible teaches.
We don't pretend to have all the answers or to get
everything right. Our liberal friends have called us
bigots. Our conservative friends have accused us of
denying the gospel. I don't believe either is true, but
I understand why they say those things. In the midst
of it all, I pray that at the very least we will be able
to learn how to love each other. I don't believe this
is an issue that should warrant division and hostility.
We can disagree, and disagree passionately. But we

must love and respect one another as fellow followers
of Christ.

As Christians, where will we choose to make our stand? We
must choose wisely because there are significant consequences
for our own spiritual lives and those of countless others.
Clearly, our best guide is the Bible. We stand firmly on what
the Scriptures say and hold everything else loosely.

No matter how much we want it to be so, the Bible cannot be honestly engineered to say that the gay lifestyle is
consistent with Christian discipleship. But neither does it
say that being gay somehow specially singles out gays and
lesbians for God's judgment.

Judging by the way homosexuality is spoken of by many
in the church, we get the idea that it is tantamount to the
"unpardonable sin," but that is not the case. Not even close.
The Bible reserves its strongest words for things such as greed,
hatred, and lack of concern for the poor. The story of the
destruction of Sodom and Gomorrah (Genesis 18 and 19)
is often cited as the irrefutable example of God's judgment
on homosexuality. But is it? Ezekiel 16:49 reveals something
interesting: "This was the guilt of your sister Sodom: she
and her daughters had arrogance, abundant food and careless ease, but she did not help the poor and needy" (NASB).
The overarching issue in God's eyes appears to be Sodom's
haughty indifference to the plight of the suffering that arose
from their comfort and excess. It could be said that gluttony
and pride destroyed Sodom.

This is not to say that homosexuality is not an issue.

According to Romans 1, it is. But it is not the *primary* issue. In Romans 1, homosexuality is mentioned alongside such issues as envy, strife, gossip and slander, lack of love and mercy, even disobedience to parents (Romans 1:29-31). The point of this portion of Scripture is that these are things that God has "given us over to"—they are a consequence of God's judgment on our rebellion against him. It simply will not do to single out homosexuality as necessitating its own specialized condemnation. Our slander, gossip, and lack of love and mercy are just as consequential. In fact, Paul says as much at the beginning of Romans 2. He warns us against taking a judgmental posture that is lacking in mercy because we, too, are guilty of being out of step with God's intention for our lives. The entire human race finds itself in the same boat of culpability, and thus we must extend God's kindness, mercy, and patience to *all* of his people. Jesus died for *all* our sins. To deny God's mercy to our gay and lesbian family, friends, and neighbors is to deny the sufficiency of the blood of Jesus for ourselves. In our judgment, we place ourselves under the judgment of God.

This brings Jesus' summation of the law of God into greater focus. When he was asked to name the greatest commandment, he replied, "'Love the Lord your God with all your heart and with all your soul and with all your mind.' This is the first and greatest commandment. And the second is like it: 'Love your neighbor as yourself.' All the Law and the Prophets hang on these two commandments" (Matthew 22:37-40). The apostle Paul says the same thing—that in loving one another, we fulfill the law of God (Romans 13:8, 10;

Galatians 5:14). Jesus said that this love between his people is central to our Christian identity (John 13:35). So we don't have to agree with our gay brothers and sisters in Christ, but at the very least we have to love them *as brothers and sisters in Christ*. Failure to love makes our lives contrary to that of Jesus. It's messy and confusing, I know. But such is the way of following Jesus into the briarpatch.

ALL IN

The 1997 sci-fi movie *Gattaca* is the story of two brothers born at a time when reproductive and genetic technologies are commonly used to minimize congenital disorders and enhance desirable human characteristics and capacities. The elder brother, Vincent, is conceived without the aid of eugenics, and thus has a high probability of developing mental and physical disorders.

Regretting their earlier decision to forgo the use of technology, Vincent's parents utilize genetic selection in conceiving their second child, Anton, who proves to be superior to his older brother.

As part of their natural rivalry while growing up, the boys play a game they call "chicken," in which they swim as far as they can out to sea. The first to give up and return to shore is the loser. The first time they swim, Anton wins, due to his superior physical stamina, and Vincent is reminded of his genetic inferiority.

When they are older, Vincent challenges Anton to another game of chicken. This time, Vincent swims farther out than his brother. When Anton falters and begins to drown, he has to be rescued by his genetically deficient older brother. Their relationship has clearly changed.

Toward the end of the story, Anton and Vincent swim against each other again, and again Vincent wins. When Anton asks Vincent how he managed to beat him—not only once, but twice—Vincent replies, "I never saved anything for the swim back."

This is how we must enter the briarpatch, not saving our strength or constantly marking our path for the return, but committed to go as deep as it takes, giving all of our strength to love. If we are to love as Jesus calls us to, in the mystery and the mess, we must be willing to go all in, not saving anything for the swim back.

Living and loving amid the pain and alienation of the briarpatch does not require us to be spiritually elite in some way, but only to have the heart and courage to trust God and keep going. It's not easy; in fact, at times it can be downright terrifying; but unless we are willing to push the boundaries of love and reconciliation, we will always turn back.

In the book of 1 John, the apostle writes to men and women in and around the city of Ephesus who are from incredibly diverse backgrounds. As a major trade route, Ephesus was a multinational, multiethnic city. As the site of the temple to Artemis, it was a place of religious pluralism, temple prostitutes, and those who had no faith commitment at all. At the very beginning of the book, John says, "We have seen this Jesus with our own eyes and touched him with our own hands. . . . In him we have fellowship with God and with one another" (1 John 1:1, 3, my paraphrase). One thing that defines the reality of Jesus, whom the apostles saw and touched, is his ability to take diverse people and bring them into intimate fellowship *with one another*. He makes us family—God's family—with all of our ethnic, political, social, and lifestyle diversity, not by religious ritual but by our common profession of faith in Jesus, who "purifies us from all sin" (1 John 1:7).

Notice again, we do not have to agree with one another in order to love one another. It's not hard to imagine the pluralistic Ephesian church having significant disagreements. Yet they still shared fellowship in Christ with one another. To say that we will only maintain relationships with people who agree with us is biblically unsupportable, not to mention intellectually dishonest and relationally unfair. Nobody lives that way. Nobody ever agrees with everyone else on all major issues. If we are honest, we often don't even know if we agree with ourselves—we change our own views from time to time. Are we going to abandon our circle of relationships every time a difference or disagreement arises?

Mark 9 records an extraordinary scene in which some of Jesus' disciples see a man casting out demons in Jesus' name and try to stop him "because he was not one of us" (Mark 9:38). They opposed him because he was not a part of their circle. Jesus' response is surprising: "Do not stop him. . . . Whoever is not against us is for us" (Mark 9:39-40).

The relational net that Jesus casts is astonishingly broad. He doesn't say, "Whoever is not for us is against us," which in our vernacular would mean, "Whoever does not agree with everything we believe must be against us." Rather, he says, "Whoever is not against us is for us." He allows for very liberal inclusion and diversity within the family of his followers. Christians have the unfortunate habit of viewing anyone who does not agree with their secondary and tertiary doctrines or issues as being their theological or spiritual enemy. But Jesus essentially says, "Anyone who claims my name must be received." A plain extrapolation might go something like this: Anyone who believes in my life, death, and resurrection and seeks to follow me, however imperfectly, is part of the family.

Jesus calls us to go further than we are typically comfortable going, to swim out much farther than we think our relational or theological strength can bear. And the waters aren't smooth. It often feels as if we will be sucked under by the crosscurrents of cultural accommodation and antagonism. When we have the courage to follow Jesus, we find that the waters of his affection and grace prove to be far less discriminating and far more uninhibited than we ever expected.

EQUAL OPPORTUNITY OFFENDER

By this point, everyone is typically frustrated or even offended. When we say that the active gay lifestyle is inconsistent with Christian discipleship, our progressive friends object to such a narrow-minded statement. But as Richard B. Hays, dean of the Duke Divinity School, argues in his book *The Moral Vision of the New Testament*, Scripture simply can't be made to support a harmonization of homosexual relationships and obedience to God's commands.

On the other hand, neither does the Bible support the condemnation and vitriol that is often directed at the gay and lesbian community by those who are followers of Christ. The Bible nowhere says that being gay relegates people to hell or disqualifies them for membership in the family of God. Only a rejection of the person and work of Jesus does that. "There is now no condemnation for those who are in Christ Jesus" (Romans 8:1) is a truth that we hold dear, but we take pause in applying it to our disputes over human sexuality. We are, paradoxically, offended by the liberal grace of the gospel when it calls us to venture into such turbulent and uncharted waters of grace.

So now that everyone is offended, what do we do?

Well, for starters, we need not be surprised by our indignation.

Jesus did a lot of offending during his earthly ministry. He offended both the religious and the secular with his claims to be God and King. He offended the rich by calling them to put him above their possessions. He offended the sensibilities of many by eating with tax collectors and thieves and defending a woman on the brink of being stoned to death for adultery. So in our wrestling with issues of sexuality, we are in good company.

We are offended that God does not sanction the openly gay lifestyle. Or we are offended that he does not give us the freedom to exclude our gay and lesbian brothers and sisters from the family. Such is life in the tangled briarpatch of God's holiness and grace, where Jesus calls us to live.

So what is the answer?

I honestly don't know. This particular path through the briarpatch is a scary one for me, too, and it does not seem that God has given us clear direction in the Scripture for clearing up the tension.

Nevertheless, to my gay brothers and sisters in Christ, please hear me: If you are a follower of Jesus, the grace of God is for you and nothing can separate you from his deep affection. We are part of the same family and I count it a privilege to worship God alongside you. I don't think the Bible supports same-sex relationships, but that does not mean I think you love Jesus less than I do in my own struggles with things the Bible clearly speaks against—greed, unforgiveness, or even lust. It just means we are all sinners in need of the grace God provides for us in the cross of Jesus. Brokenness is in all of us. We are in this together. We are family.

I realize this may sound too simplistic. Life—your life—is far more complicated than that; but perhaps it's a place to start. I welcome a generous and compassionate dialogue as we plumb the depths of God's grace together.

To my friends who struggle with being compassionate toward the gay community, remember that the grace of Christ in which you rest does not depend on your ability to measure up. If you're being honest, there are many areas in your own life in which you're not even trying to obey or conform to God's commands. Your only hope is the mercy of God in Christ. Make room for your gay brothers and sisters to stand on that same foundation of mercy with you.

REFLECTION AND REFRACTION

My neighbor James and I became friends. We talked out on the street and enjoyed hanging out at parties and with gatherings of friends. We picked up each other's mail and newspaper when the other was out of town. We had lunch together occasionally and were a part of the same Bible study. We worshiped together and taught one another more about what it looked like to follow Jesus. I mocked his affinity for Cher and he mocked my affinity for cigars, but a genuine affection grew between us.

I learned more about James's spiritual journey and the conflict his homosexuality had caused in his family and his church. His history was a tragic one of rejection and wrong assumptions that left him alienated from the people he loved the most and from the church in which he had been raised and taught to love Jesus.

One day we were having lunch downtown and began talking about church. After being a part of our congregation for more than a year, he heard about our denominational affiliation and was surprised. Poking his fork at his salad (James is a health freak), he glanced up at me and said, "You know, I was raised in this same denomination. My father was an elder. When I came out, it was terrible. Had I known our church was in the same denomination, I never would have walked through the doors."

"Really?" I said. "That's too bad."

"Yeah, but now it's too late because this is my family. I feel so loved by these people, even though I know many of them don't agree with my lifestyle."

James was experiencing the sometimes unsettling nature of the simultaneous *reflection* and *refraction* of the gospel.

We are to be like mirrors of the gospel, reflecting the real presence of Jesus for anyone who is looking. We cannot say we believe we are saved by grace if we are not willing to reflect the same grace to others. This doesn't mean we have to hide our convictions about what the Bible says about how we should live our lives; but it does mean that we take what the Bible says about love with equal seriousness. The Bible gives us a picture of what "reflection" looks like: "Be completely humble and gentle; be patient, bearing with one another in love. Make every effort to keep the unity of the Spirit through the bond of peace" (Ephesians 4:2-3). Humility and gentleness are primary reflections of the reality of Christ.

The gospel is not only to be reflected in the way we love with humility and gentleness; it also alters our view of life. It causes us to see things differently—a *refraction*, if you will.

Take a straw and put it into a glass of water. When viewed from a certain angle, it will appear to bend at the water's surface. That's refraction. When we view life through the medium of the gospel, it gives us a new way of seeing. It provides an understanding of life with God that is different from that of the musk ox ("God will love you only if you keep the rules") or the chameleon ("Never mind what God says; we will make our own rules"). Neither of these perspectives is acceptable for us as Christians because we have been given the refractive lenses of the gospel. God is real. He is holy and his commandments matter. We do not have the freedom to make our own rules. And yet his grace bends to accommodate our warped and broken lives, whether gay or straight.

Your capacity to reflect the gospel of Christ in love, humility, and gentleness will depend on how deeply his grace has refracted your heart. If you struggle to see how God's mercy bends to give you grace for all of your foolishness, you will likewise struggle to reflect his mercy to others who live in ways with which you disagree or who disagree with the way you live.

IN THIS TOGETHER

As a preacher, I have grown accustomed to post-sermon critiques. Even the most prudent speaker will sooner or later misspeak, saying something that is insensitive, theologically wrong, or just plain stupid. When you speak for a living, it's just a matter of time before you offend someone through careless words or an honest mistake. I do this more often than I care to admit.

So I wasn't surprised when Thomas, whom I had never met, walked up to me after church one Sunday with tears in his eyes.

It must have been a big one. I made this guy cry!

"You mentioned in your sermon how gay people are called to follow Jesus just like everyone else, that they are not on a separate path of obedience and grace just because they are gay. You said the gospel of Christ is the same for all of us."

Uncertain from which direction his question would eventually come, I played my cards close to the chest. "Uh, yeah. That sounds about right."

"I have been a Christian for more than thirty years and am a gay man," he said. "In all of those years, I have never heard a preacher even acknowledge that I was here. You made me feel like I was wanted, like I belonged in the family of God, without making me feel either dirty or privileged because of my sexuality. Thank you."

Friends, if Jesus is real—and he is—he must be real for all of us, and we are all called to share together—as one family—in his work of grace among us. We are, by far, more alike in our struggle to obey his commands and our need for his radical affection than we realize. We fail God and we fail one another if we do not learn how to both challenge and love one another in a manner that reflects God's material presence in our lives. It's not easy, but I can tell you from experience, it's worth the effort.

TRANSFORMING
THE BRIARPATCH

CHAPTER 11

OPEN BORDERS
LIVING OUTSIDE
THE WALLS

"Everyone who calls on the name of the Lord
will be saved." How, then, can they call on the
one they have not believed in? And how can
they believe in the one of whom they have
not heard? And how can they hear without
someone preaching to them? And how can
anyone preach unless they are sent? As it is
written: "How beautiful are the feet of those
who bring good news!"

ROMANS 10:13-15

I am a pastor—a professional Christian—so I spend a lot of
time with Jesus. I'm not saying my work is any more spiritual
than that of a lawyer, teacher, or store clerk; I firmly believe
that we are all called to reflect the grace, love, and mercy of
Jesus in our vocational lives—whether by righting an injustice, loving a child who comes from a broken or neglectful
home, or being kind and helpful to every customer—because
these things are the stuff of God's Kingdom. We are called to
model the hope and healing of the gospel of Jesus Christ in
all we do, including our work.

While most people spend their weeks preparing cases,

teaching algebra, stocking shelves, or caring for children, I write sermons (about Jesus), plan ministries, visit people in the hospital, and counsel individuals and couples in the principles of the Kingdom life. I am often up to my neck in spiritual stuff that, honestly, does not seem to know the meaning of "office hours." It oozes into the weekends and the wee hours of the night. It's work that is every bit as relentless as it is rewarding, but being a pastor is like any other job: Sometimes I really look forward to quittin' time, clocking out. "See ya Monday, Jesus. Have a good weekend."

Sometimes, I need to not be a pastor just for a little while and not talk to anyone about God or think about church. I know that sounds faithless and selfish and spiritually weak—which are all true—but there are times when I want to take off the proverbial clerical collar and call it a day. And I wish Jesus would do the same.

But he doesn't clock out. As followers of Jesus, we are called to "always be prepared to give an answer to everyone who asks [us] to give the reason for the hope that [we] have" (1 Peter 3:15). In a sense, we are always on call, and the pager goes off at the weirdest, most unexpected times. But all Jesus asks is that we report for duty, be ourselves, and enter the briarpatch.

One such day came for me about eight years ago. It was late summer and we were in the throes of getting our new church off the ground. The days were long and exhausting and I needed a break, so I made plans to meet a couple of friends at the Brick Store Pub in Decatur after work. I was looking forward to it all day.

At the time, my friends were starting a music magazine that had already gotten a lot of attention and great reviews, and we had just started a softball team in the city rec league, so we had a lot of stuff to talk about—fun stuff, normal stuff. Along with their families, they were also a part of our new church, so we unavoidably talked about that as well.

Sigh.

During the course of our conversation about church stuff, it became obvious that the stranger sitting to my left was interested in what we were saying.

"You guys are talking about church," he interjected. "Are you preachers or somethin'?"

I looked over to my friends and said nothing.

They looked at me. They looked back at the stranger. They looked at one another and then simultaneously pointed at me and said, "Nope. But he is." They promptly asked for their check, and before I knew it, I was alone with this stranger.

Thanks, guys. Back on the clock.

He wasted no time before launching into a profanity-laced assault on all things religious, the gist of which was something like this: "I hate God. He's never done a single thing for me."

Okay. This is going to be fun. I figured some of his aggression came from the fact that he was on his fourth or fifth whiskey and Coke. "Liquid courage," as they say. But I knew there was some deep pain beneath the anger.

I turned on my stool to face him, ordered myself a drink, and settled in for what promised to be a long conversation.

"Tell me more," I invited. "I can take it, and I'm pretty sure God can too."

For the next hour, Dan dominated the conversation as he recounted not knowing his father and being raised by a mother who was loveless and neglectful. She brought into their home countless boyfriends who would beat her, as well as Dan and his younger sister.

When he was old enough, he moved out and found his way to Los Angeles, where he got involved in the pornography industry. He was successful enough to earn a living and support many destructive habits. Involvement in that industry was not conducive to healthy, long-term relationships, so he burned through a string of girlfriends and countless one-night stands.

I kept listening. He kept talking and ordering more drinks. It was one of the saddest stories I had ever heard, and I had the sense that he had never told it to anyone before. I thought it could not get any worse.

I was wrong.

"So what brings you to Decatur?" His story had caught up to the present, and honestly, I was hoping my question would change the subject.

"I'm here to testify in my mother's murder trial." He pointed across the square in the general direction of the county courthouse.

My jaw dropped and I began to think, *Yeah, I can see why you're not God's biggest fan.*

"My mother didn't like my sister's boyfriend," he continued. "He would beat my sister, and so my mom got a gun and went and shot him dead."

I was done. Exhausted.

We sat in silence for a few minutes, staring into our respective drinks.

He raised his whiskey and Coke to his mouth and muttered into the glass, "So you'll excuse me if I think God is full of it."

More silence.

"You know what I think?" I finally said, not waiting for an answer. "I think you've been deserted and neglected by those who should have loved and protected you. Your father had no right to leave. That's not what fathers are supposed to do. Sure, your mother had it bad, but she had a responsibility to protect you and your sister. She let you down. And correct me if I am wrong, but by the way you're tossing down so much whiskey, beginning at four in the afternoon, I think you're an alcoholic. You're looking for meaning and belonging in an industry and illicit relationships that are only emaciating your soul. But deep down, beneath the porn and drugs and abuse and alcohol, your real problem is that you don't think anyone can love you, not even God. You don't think God could possibly love someone like you."

He sat there, head slumped, long enough for the tears to reach his chin. Raising his eyes, he looked at me and said, "You know, you're right."

"Dan, the truth is, if God can't love you, then there's no hope for me either. A lot of bad stuff has happened to you, but you've made some pretty bad decisions yourself. The good news is that none of that disqualifies you for God's affection. Jesus came for broken and stupid people just like you and me. And it's not fair for us to blame God for everything if we are going to purposely shut him out of our lives. When you sober up a bit and get back to LA tomorrow, I want you to call a friend of mine."

I gave him the phone number and he promised he would call. He shook my hand and pulled me in for a hug. "Thank you," he said. "For the first time in my life, I think someone could love me. Maybe even God."

The gospel is not just for those who can muster the strength to go to church or pray or attend a Bible study. It's not just for those who have their moral, religious, or relational ducks in a row. The gospel is also for the most prickly and broken among us—those for whom the idea that God could be loving, accepting, forgiving, and accessible is utterly foreign. We must introduce them to this God and to his deep affection displayed in the life, death, and resurrection of Jesus.

For any such introduction to be possible, though, we must be willing to live beyond the walls of our churches and outside of our relational foxholes. I like my job, a lot. But pastors don't have a monopoly on caring for the spiritually broken and bruised. We can't leave the work to the "professional Christians." We all must be willing to walk into the briarpatch with confidence and courage, knowing that Jesus will meet us there, even if we have never preached a sermon or graduated from seminary. We need not ask for the check and settle up our tab when things get deep and prickly. If Jesus had intended for the hard cases to be handled only by the credentialed and qualified, he would have done everything himself. But he didn't. He poured himself into others and sent them out. They were fishermen, tax guys, and common laborers who were not especially faithful and did not feel particularly qualified. And they went into their cities and neighborhoods—not as professional spiritual know-it-alls, but as imperfect men and women who had seen Jesus and in whom his presence was unrelenting—to speak the healing affection of God into the fractured lives all around them. The world has not been the same since.

We must embrace the reality that we are always on call—the pursuing mercy of Jesus does not rest; he never clocks out. The borders of God's Kingdom—the Kingdom that encompasses the briarpatch of sin and stupidity, brokenness and brutality all around us—are wide open. Anyone can enter. Anyone—bankers and blasphemers, professors and pornographers. We must remember that the most religious and righteous, prickly and pugnacious among us were once outside the Kingdom of God's grace and have been welcomed in through faith in Jesus (Ephesians 2:1-10). The offer of grace in the gospel is liberal and free, giving us the hope and courage to flourish in the briarpatch as we point our fellow human beings to the life of God.

Do you believe that?

FREE GRACE
One Sunday after church, a friend approached and wanted to introduce me to her neighbor, who was visiting for the first time.

"This is Mary. She lives a couple doors down from us."

"Hi." I shook her hand. "Nice to meet you."

"I really liked the service," she volunteered. "The music was well done. The prayers were beautiful and everyone has been so friendly."

"I am so glad to hear that," I said.

"But I didn't really care for the sermon."

Bold. I like it. "What, particularly, didn't you like?"

"It was all fine, except for the part about Jesus being the only way to God. That got emphasized a lot and I find it to be exclusive and arrogant to say such a thing." She continued, "What about my Hindu friends? They are the nicest people you will ever meet. I believe in Jesus, but who says *they* have to? I have a problem with anyone saying they are out just because they don't believe in Jesus."

"I hear what you're saying," I said, "but your problem is not with me. Your problem is with Jesus. I'm not the one who made the exclusive claims. Jesus himself said, 'I am the way, the truth, and the life. No one can come to the Father except through me.'"[1]

Not satisfied, she replied, "I still think it is arrogant to say that Jesus is the only way. All religions are the same. They are just different paths to the same God."

Of course, the statement that all religions are essentially the same is itself a claim of exclusivity, and is more arrogant than anything Jesus ever said. But rather than simply point this out to Mary, I told her a parable that has its roots in first-century Buddhist writings. It goes something like this:

There once were six blind men who were asked to determine what an elephant was like. The first man

touched the elephant's leg and said the elephant
is like a pillar. The second touched its tail and
determined that an elephant is like a rope. The third
touched its trunk and likened the elephant to a
strong branch. The fourth touched an ear and said
an elephant is like a large hand fan. The fifth, feeling
the large belly, said it was like a wall. The last man
grabbed one of the elephant's tusks and compared
the elephant to a solid pipe.

Which one was correct?

As the parable is told, they were all correct. Each man's experience, though different from the others', was an equally valid interpretation of the elephant. But because the men were blind, they were unable to see the full reality of the elephant. So it is with the world's religions. They are each correct in their own right, but all suffer from the handicap of not being able to see the full truth. Thus, it is arrogant and foolish for any one religion to claim it is true or exclusive. Such was Mary's assertion.

But as I pointed out to her, the teller of the parable assumes for himself (or herself) the ability to see the whole elephant, thus claiming an exclusive, all-knowing perspective that is denied to everyone else. To apply it to religious belief is to claim a superior place of "true" knowledge that is denied to every other religious belief. To assert that each of the world's religions sees only part of the truth is to claim for ourselves a view of the whole truth. How fair is that?

The reality is that every faith, not just Christianity, believes theirs to be the true truth. As G. K. Chesterton said, "Every day one comes across somebody who says that of course his view may not be the right one. Of course his view must be the right one, or it is not his view."² Christianity is not arrogant for claiming truth because everyone thinks their own view is best, or at least *more* true than the other views, or there would be no intellectual integrity in holding their view. That is simply the nature of believing anything.

The uniqueness and beauty of Christianity come not because it claims to be true, but because of *what* it claims. And those unique claims begin and end with Jesus.

Christianity asserts that Jesus Christ has come as God in the flesh (1 John 4:2). Jesus *came*. He was somewhere else before he was here. His being is eternal, before time, transcending human reality. He showed up on the scene and announced himself to be the incarnation of God himself (John 14:9). No other major world religion claims divinity for its leader. They were all human and *only* human. Christianity alone asserts that in Jesus, God has come into the world.

C. S. Lewis writes, "There is no parallel in other religions. If you had gone to Buddha and asked him, 'Are you the son of Bramah?' he would have said, 'My son, you are still in the vale of illusion.' If you had gone to Socrates and asked, 'Are you Zeus?' he would have laughed at you. If you had gone to Muhammad and asked, 'Are you Allah?' he would first have rent his clothes and then cut your head off."³

Jesus claims to be God. This alone separates Christianity from every other faith.

But *why* did he come?

Other religions seek to escape the flesh and the world because both are deemed irredeemably corrupt. But in Jesus, God came to *inhabit* the flesh. He was "born of a woman," born into the physical reality of human form. Why? "To redeem those [of us] under the law, that we might receive adoption" as heirs (Galatians 4:5). Jesus did not come to abolish the flesh or the material world; he came to redeem it! Christianity does not seek to eradicate who we are; it seeks, through the redemption of Jesus, to bring us more fully into who we were created to be—physical beings full of beauty, peace, and harmony—in accord with God, ourselves, others, and all of creation. Jesus came to fix what is broken in humanity (you and me) and in the world. He came to eliminate death, poverty, oppression, loneliness, hatred, injustice, and the countless other maladies that have corrupted human existence.

Christianity alone has the theological foundation from which to seek the peace and prosperity of the world, and reconciliation and harmony among humanity and all of creation. This is utterly unique to the claims and ministry of Jesus. No other religion promises the redemption of the world—*this* world, the one we all live in.

Over and above all else, what distinguishes Christianity from the world's religions is the radical, liberal, and free grace of Jesus Christ offered to anyone and everyone who will believe. We don't have to deny our faults. We don't have to keep the rules in order to be accepted by God or try harder in order to be loved. Only Christianity dares to make God's love completely unconditional. Christ died for us, not *after* we got our moral ducks in a row, but "while we were still sinners" (Romans 5:8). While we were spiritually dead in our foolishness and rebellion, God gave us his grace and affection in Jesus (Ephesians 2:1-10).

Why does something as seemingly simple and innocuous as *grace* matter?

If we believe we are "saved" (that is, loved and accepted by God) because of our religious or moral performance, then we have a couple of major, recurring hurdles to get over. First, we're not even able to keep our own moral standards, much less God's. Assuming we believe that things such as lying, cheating, sexual impropriety, or screaming out at someone in anger are wrong, we most certainly recognize that we do wrong. At least occasionally, if not regularly. And this says nothing about God's standards and desires for us. If we cannot keep our own standards, we cannot hope to keep God's. As a result, we will live in a constant state of guilt and fear. We could try harder to be a better person, but that only digs us in deeper. Failure to live up to our own standards is a crushing and discouraging cycle that will ultimately make us bitter and devoid of grace in our lives.

Second, if our righteousness is based on our moral performance, we must see ourselves as superior to others because we are at least *trying* to be good. We will inevitably look down our self-righteous noses at those who make no effort to please God or obey his commands. But the gospel of grace is the only posture of belief that assures us that we are no better than anyone else—even an alcoholic porn actor. Why? Because to have the gospel in our lives, we must admit that we are sinners in need of grace. Only the gospel of Jesus Christ humbles us before the stark reality of our need for grace.

This astounding reality of our need for grace is why things like coercion, hatred, bigotry, arrogance, or violence are antithetical to the message of Jesus and have no place in the lives of his followers. We must be people who rest in the grace of Christ, knowing that if God can love and forgive people like us, he can love and forgive anyone, anytime, anyplace. Period. Those who practice cruelty and condescension in the name of Christianity simply do not understand Christianity.

Theologian Lesslie Newbigin speaks of the peace of grace that is central to faith in Jesus, a peace that must ripple out beyond our communities of faith.

> There is a longing for unity among all human
> beings, for unity offers the promise of peace. The
> problem is that we want unity on our terms, and it
> is our rival programs for unity which tear us apart.
> As Augustine said, all wars are fought for the sake
> of peace. The history of the world could be told
> as the story of successive efforts to bring unity to
> the world, and of course the name we give to these
> efforts is "imperialism." The Christian gospel has
> sometimes been made the tool of an imperialism,
> and of that we have to repent. But at its heart is the
> denial of all imperialisms, *for at its center there is
> the cross where all imperialisms are humbled and we
> are invited to find the center of human unity in the
> One who was made nothing so that all might be one.*

> The very heart of the biblical vision for the unity
> of humankind is that its center is not an imperial
> power but the slain Lamb.[4]

Friends, Jesus is the only way to God. That is his exclusive, undeniable claim. But Christianity is actually the most *inclusive* faith because in Jesus, the grace and peace of God is offered to all, without exception—religious and irreligious, rich and poor, weak and powerful, sinners, fools, and failures. "For God so loved the world that he gave his one and only Son, that whoever believes in him shall not perish but have eternal life" (John 3:16).

The gospel of God's grace in Jesus Christ must be for everyone. If not, there is no hope for anyone. Will we have the courage to step out of our bunkers of self-righteousness and bring that grace and hope to those who need it just as much as we do?

GET OUT OF TENNESSEE

My grandmother was one of the strongest and most loving people I have ever met. Eager to shower affection on her brood of grandchildren, she was the unquestioned matriarch of our family and seemed to hold everyone together through the sheer force of her will. No matter the conflict or difficulty in each of our lives, her presence was a comforting and stabilizing force. And behind her titanic heart was a backbone of steel. To this day, she is the only person I've ever seen my father acquiesce to. As a kid, I was in awe of her. Surely she had some sort of deep magic or ninja skills. Maybe she was a Jedi in support hose and pearls? Regardless, she certainly enjoyed her reputation for toughness and went out of her way to foster an image of being a "hard-core granny," even down to the car she drove.

Her ride was a 1974 Monte Carlo that would outrun most of the muscle cars in her urban neighborhood. The fact that she scarcely exceeded thirty miles per hour and only drove to church or the grocery store didn't really matter. The important thing was that she *could* leave most everyone in the dust if she wanted to. She knew it, and she knew that everyone else knew it. She was an enigma and enjoyed every minute of it.

Her front license plate read, "Follow me to Tennessee" and was yet another of the paradoxes that surrounded this small, strong woman. To my knowledge, she rarely left the state of Tennessee and her car never left metro Nashville. Most people who would have been able to read the license plate would have been walking through the parking lot of Bordeaux Church of Christ or the Piggly Wiggly, both of which were firmly within the borders of the state of Tennessee. How could they follow her to Tennessee if they were already *in* Tennessee? For it to be a valid, meaningful overture, she would have to get out of Tennessee. Otherwise, it was an empty invitation.

As Christians, we often do a similar thing. We want to "lead people to Jesus," yet we never leave the confines of our privatized Christian subculture and go into the places where the vast majority of our neighbors live and play. If we want them to follow Jesus, we have to "get out of Tennessee," outside the borders of church, Sunday school, potlucks, and insular Christian relationships.

At our church, we intentionally keep "church activities" to a bare minimum. We meet together for worship on Sunday mornings and encourage everyone to join a community group that meets during the week. We understand the importance of Christian fellowship, but we also know we can easily have too much of a good thing, to the detriment of our larger community. For that reason, we encourage our folks to get to know their neighbors, throw parties in their homes, get involved in their children's schools, and serve the needy in our city. In other words, "get out of Tennessee."

This is precisely what Jesus did. Sure, he attended synagogue and spent lots of time with his disciples, but he spent even more time outside the borders of religious practice where his invitation to "follow me" actually made sense. He did this from the very beginning of his ministry.

> After John was put in prison, Jesus went into Galilee, proclaiming the good news of God. "The time has come," he said. "The kingdom of God has come near. Repent and believe the good news!"
>
> As Jesus walked beside the Sea of Galilee, he saw Simon and his brother Andrew casting a net into the lake, for they were fishermen. "Come, follow me," Jesus said, "and I will send you out to fish for people." At once they left their nets and followed him.
>
> MARK 1:14-18

Throughout the New Testament, God's Kingdom is spoken of as something to be *entered*, and the invitation is given to those outside the borders—the broken and poor, the marginalized and contrite, the little children. The "good news," says Jesus, is that the Kingdom of God is near for the taking. In Jesus, the Kingdom makes a personal appearance. The Kingdom has broken in, but it seems we only get a taste. We experience it now in the person of Jesus, but its fullness has yet to be revealed. There is more to come.

When I was a teenager, a friend of my father's hired me to dig up the stump of a small tree in front of his house. At least I *thought* it was a small tree, and the price of thirty dollars seemed like a great deal. I started early in the morning and fully expected to be finished in little more than an hour.

I quickly discovered that the stump was just the tip. The roots ran deeper, and were more numerous than I would ever have imagined. It took literally all day for me to unearth most of the roots, leaving many untouched (and, I hoped, unnoticed) beneath the surface.

When Jesus announces the nearness of the Kingdom of God, he is saying, "In me you see the stump, but the roots of redemption and wholeness are yet to be unearthed." It would be years before even the disciples would understand the depth of what Jesus meant. In fact, the fullness of the Kingdom of which he spoke is yet to be seen; but the incarnation of Jesus is the beginning of the final in-breaking of God into human history. The Kingdom is near. That is the good news that Jesus embodies and proclaims.

In Mark 13:28, Jesus tells his disciples about the full fruition of the Kingdom. He says, "Now learn this lesson from the fig tree: As soon as its twigs get tender and its leaves come out, you know that summer is near." The fullness of summer is coming next. The time Jesus spent on earth was the sign that the fullness of God's Kingdom would be the next thing.

THE INVITATION

This idea of nearness carries a sense of urgency. Jesus says, "The kingdom of God has come near. Repent and believe the good news! . . . Come, follow me" (Mark 1:15, 17).

Notice, he doesn't say, "If you are a good person, follow me." He says nothing about performing religious rituals or making amends for wrongs before being qualified to follow him. He says, simply, "Repent. Believe the good news." Repentance is more an expression of dependence than it is self-deprecation. Sure, it involves acknowledging that we are sinners, but pretty much everyone freely admits they do wrong stuff all the time. Admitting that we do wrong is not repentance. It's honesty. Repentance is realizing that we need Jesus to show us the way to God. More precisely, repentance is looking to Jesus to *be* our way to God. And he can be that way for anyone, no matter how deep their sin or self-righteousness runs. The borders are open and the vacancy sign is on. Repentance is as simple as walking through the door and claiming our room.

Is this the message we send in our churches, among our friends and coworkers, to our friends and neighbors, or to people we meet at the park or in the pub? Are we letting them know their room is ready and waiting for them? Are we even aware of the subconscious signals we transmit that subtly undermine the simple and free invitation of Jesus? "This is how a follower of Jesus dresses. This is what a real Christian looks like, smells like, talks like." Are we expecting folks to deal with their thorns of brokenness before following us into the Kingdom, lest they inadvertently prick and puncture our veneer of polite religious practice? Are we making it more complicated than Jesus did?

He says, "Acknowledge the ways you have made a mess of your life. See that you have tried to be the lord of your own life and that has not worked out as well as you had hoped. Admit your need for grace and forgiveness."

And then, "Believe the good news." The Greek word that Mark uses for "good news" in recording what Jesus said is *euangelion*, which in the first century had deep cultural and historic meaning. It referred to history-shaping, life-altering news, not just everyday news. Prior to the coming of Jesus, *euangelion* had no religious meaning to speak of.

In the first century, *euangelion* or *gospel* referred to the birth and coronation of the ruler namely, Caesar Augustus—who brought freedom, peace, and prosperity to his people. In ancient Greece, when battles were won, heralds were sent back to the people to proclaim a "gospel": "Your army has won victory for you. You are free." A "gospel" is the story of a history-shaping event that changed everything on behalf of the people.

This is the gospel that we are called to bring to our communities, neighborhoods, and workplaces: Jesus has come for *you*. He lived and died for *you*, so that you may be reconciled to God, regardless of your history, your pain, or your struggles.

The gospel of Jesus Christ is for anyone who dares to believe that God could love someone like them, that he really is a savior who welcomes lepers, prostitutes, rebels, thieves, orphans, and even self-righteous clergy. Such are the stones that make up the temple of God, and such are the people we want among us in the family of faith. We welcome them gladly, thorns and all, because we delight in seeing the grace of God enfold, heal, and transform their broken and bludgeoned lives. If the grace of God is not for them, there is no hope for any of us.

This requires the courage to live outside the walls of a privatized faith, where the foolish and the fractured live. It means that we must always remember the undeserved grace and forgiveness that God has given us. Unfortunately, we too easily forget the unmerited affection of God.

When my kids were little, it was common for them to make their way into our bedroom in the middle of the night and climb into bed with us when they had bad dreams or just couldn't sleep. It was not an unwanted interruption but a true delight to wrap our arms around them in love. This is what loving parents do for their children. And it's what God does for us when we turn to him. He soothes us, protects us, and reassures us of his love.

The truth is, God really likes being God. He likes being *your* God. He loves his job and doesn't see any drudgery or inconvenience in it. He doesn't wake up every morning saying, "What pathetic losers can I save from hell today?" NO! He doesn't just tolerate us like an underpaid babysitter; he delights in us like an enraptured Father. He dotes over us and writes songs about us (Zephaniah 3:17). He quiets, comforts, and emboldens us with his love. This is the reality that frees us to love others as we have been loved. This is the grace that keeps the borders to God's Kingdom wide open to the briarpatches all around us. This is the good news that bids anyone and everyone to come, repent, and dare to believe that God loves them, too.

CHAPTER 12

GETTING IN TUNE
THE HARMONY OF HEAVEN AND EARTH

Heaven is important, but it's not
the end of the world.

N. T. WRIGHT

If Dante had ever attended a middle school orchestra concert, he would certainly have added a tenth circle of hell.

I confess that I am not one to criticize musicianship. I
know about six guitar chords and can play a couple of old
Journey songs on the drums, but that's it. Growing up, I
never once heard a musical instrument played in our home.
Nobody in our family could sing a note, though that never
seemed to stop my father from torturing us in the car with
old Leon Redbone or Ray Stevens tunes. Then there was his
favorite, "Plastic Jesus," sung by Paul Newman's character in
the 1967 film *Cool Hand Luke* and later recorded by artists
as diverse as the Flaming Lips, Jack Johnson, and Billy Idol.

My father's singing was, and is, cruel and unusual auditory punishment. Had I known it was an option, I would have called the state child protective services on him.

The musical void in my life was remedied when I met and married a gifted musician. There has never been a day in our marriage without the sounds of angelic singing, piano, guitar, banjo, oboe, or clarinet. Carrie opened up for me an avenue of joy and worship I had never known, and all was well . . . until our children joined the orchestra at school.

The offending instrument in our home was the cello. Played well, the cello is among the most beautifully haunting and captivating of all instruments. In the hands of a fifth grader, however, it ranks right up there with water boarding or pulling out your toenails with a pair of pliers. And just when I thought the sonic abuse could not get worse, I attended my first middle school orchestra concert.

I was hopeful as we entered the cafeteria/auditorium. At the time, it did not occur to me that the tiled floor and painted cinder-block walls would only serve to amplify the acoustic dissonance within this rectangular acoustical death trap.

The kids filed in from a side door. We parents applauded energetically as they took their seats and began to tune (I use that word loosely) their instruments. I walked down front to snap some pictures, still unaware that what was about to be unleashed would potentially interfere with the use of all electronic devices and navigational systems.

The teacher welcomed the parents and other family members to the evening's production before turning to the students and raising his baton. From the first note, it was obvious to even my own untrained ears that something was horribly wrong. Rather than falling into harmony, instruments wrestled with one another like pit bulls over beef jerky. The squeaking and squawking was reminiscent of the exotic birdhouse at the zoo, and each percussionist had a rhythm all his own.

I looked over to my wife as if to say, "Do something!" but she only smiled, patted my knee, and said, "It's okay. They're doing fine." *And stop making that face.*

I crossed my arms and looked around to see if anyone else was praying for the loss of consciousness, but they were all smiling and taking their auditory beating in stride.

Things improved by the second song. The melody was occasionally recognizable and the rhythm stabilized somewhat. I even joined the applause and avoided another elbow to the ribs, courtesy of my ever-more-patient-and-mature wife, and she assured me, "They will get better. It just takes time."

They did get better. After a couple of years, they were almost good and the concerts bordered on being enjoyable. At the very least, having experienced the initial train wreck allowed me to appreciate and be proud of the progress they made. Looking back, I can see the glimpses of beauty and echoes of harmony scattered amidst the discord. My wife and the other parents, and presumably the orchestra director, saw something that I missed: *potential.*

There was beauty among the ruins.

Just because, as middle schoolers, they would never play in perfect harmony or reach the ideal of how the music *should* be played, it did not mean that the director and students should just lay down their instruments and give up. It was precisely the hope of the ideal that drove them to keep playing, the teacher to keep conducting, and the parents to keep listening and encouraging.

THE HOPE OF HARMONY

Let me drop some theology on you. It's important for us to understand why life in the briarpatch matters and how it is connected with the story of God's redemption and grace in the Bible. The foundation of our hope in living life amid the thorns and thistles is the resurrection of Jesus. In the Resurrection, we are given a glimpse of our ideal—the harmony of all things, toward which we are called to strive.

Every one of us endures a constant barrage of spiritual, relational, political, and cultural discord. We experience strife and division in our marriages and families. We witness corruption and greed in the workplace and sometimes even participate in it. Our friends do not meet our expectations and sometimes even stab us in the back. The tension in our neighborhoods and cities among races, social classes, religious groups, and political parties is often on the verge of exploding, and the dream of human harmony feels as if it belongs in the fantasy world of unicorns and leprechauns. We instinctively know that the dissonance all around us is not how the song of human life is meant to be played. We are off pitch, out of rhythm, and no longer following the score as written.

But just because so much of our world is out of tune—filled with jarring chords of strife, abuse, suffering, and neglect—does not mean we give up playing, any more than my kids' middle school orchestra should have given up.

The death and resurrection of Jesus has meaning beyond saving souls for heaven. In Colossians 1, we are told that Jesus is the God of creation. Everything was created by him and for him, and through the Cross all things in heaven and on earth will be reconciled to him. *All things.* Not just me, not just you, but *all of creation.*

The word translated "reconcile" in Colossians 1 means "to bring into harmony." Everything God has made will be drawn back into harmony with him. As the director of the orchestra of creation, Jesus will bring all things back into tune and rhythm—playing the score as written. The harmony of all things is the larger purpose of the Cross and empty tomb.

In the Bible, the creation and redemption of humanity is never divorced from the creation and redemption of the earth, the land, nature—the physical place God has made and we inhabit. This is what the life, death, and resurrection of Jesus is getting at. Jesus did not die and rise from the dead so we can become "better people" or live "fulfilling lives." His purpose was not so much to get us into heaven as it was to get heaven into us and into the world.

CITIZENS OF HEAVEN

In the first century, during the life and ministry of Jesus and his disciples, the Roman Empire was the dominant political and cultural force. The cities and towns in which the early Christians lived, worked, and raised their families were occupied by Rome and governed by its representatives. This was simply a reality of life, even if it was a source of resentment for most people.

Those who were able to secure Roman citizenship received all the rights, privileges, and responsibilities that went along with that status. It was precisely because the apostle Paul was a Roman citizen that he was able to appeal to Caesar when he was arrested and held by the local authorities in Caesarea. Paul had the right to have his case heard in Rome because his citizenship status trumped all other factors. In the first century, citizenship was a big deal and everybody knew it.

In Philippians 3:20, Paul reminds his readers that "our citizenship is in heaven." Our tendency is to read that and say, "Never mind with this world. Whatever happens here is not our concern. Because we're citizens of heaven, we are going to escape one day, so this world can just go down in flames." Does our citizenship in heaven absolve us from responsibility on earth or give us the freedom not to worry about the problems and brokenness that surround us every day? Knowing how important citizenship status was in the first century, is that how the recipients of Paul's letter in Philippi would have understood him?

No, and here's why.

The residents of Philippi who were lucky enough to be Roman citizens would likely never step foot in the city of Rome. They had no expectation that one day, toward the end of their lives, they would be whisked away to a nice little place in the city to be rewarded for their lifetime of faithful service to the empire. The expectation placed upon them as Roman citizens was that they would be advocates for the empire *where they lived*—that they would seek the prosperity of the empire by seeking the prosperity of Philippi. Their job was to bring Roman influence and culture to bear on their city. That's what citizenship meant.

And that is exactly the point Paul is trying to get across to the Philippians and to us: Jesus has risen and God's Kingdom has broken in. We are citizens of that Kingdom *here and now*, in this place, wherever we live. Jesus is risen and God's redemption, reconciliation, and healing have been unleashed on the world; and we, as citizens of that resurrection Kingdom, are called to be advocates and conduits of the grace that is putting the world to rights. We have a job to do: to make the life of heaven—God's Kingdom—more and more an actual, physical, earthly reality.

Bishop N. T. Wright says it well in *Surprised by Hope*: "God's new world of justice and joy, of hope for the whole earth, was launched when Jesus came out of the tomb on Easter morning, and I know that he calls his followers to live in him and by the power of his Spirit and so to be new-creation people here and now, bringing signs and symbols of the kingdom to birth on earth as in heaven."[1]

JESUS IN CAMBODIA

Lisa, a twentysomething in our church, came to me one morning and said, "I'm moving to Cambodia."

Images popped into my head of Pol Pot and the brutal Khmer Rouge, who took control of Cambodia in 1975 and removed all vestiges of Western culture, including modern medicine and agricultural practices, libraries, and religion. By most estimates, almost one-third of Cambodia's eight million people died of starvation, disease, overwork, or execution.

I had seen the movie *The Killing Fields* and was convinced this was no place for a young member of our church to live.

I asked, "Why on earth would you want to live in Cambodia?"

"I got a position with International Justice Mission," she said. "I will be working with young girls who have been rescued from brothels in Phnom Penh." I knew that Lisa had just finished her master's in social work and wanted to help victims of abuse. What I didn't know was that, according to the most conservative estimates, well over ten thousand children are trafficked in the brothels of Phnom Penh alone.[2]

Cambodia is a place of brutal dissonance, out of tune with God's desire for harmony, peace, and justice in his world. Knowing Lisa's heart for the broken and her desire to see God's healing and wholeness in the world, I should not have been surprised she would move toward the hurt. I should have known she could not pray for God's Kingdom to come here on earth as it is in heaven and then just sit back and wait for Jesus to return. The hope and promise of God's beginning his resurrection project of putting the world to rights—where little girls won't be forced into slavery—is something she wants to be a part of. Cambodia is her briarpatch.

"And besides," she said, "it will only be for a year." Six years later, she's still there.

When we follow Jesus in praying, "Your kingdom come," this is what we are praying for (Matthew 6:10). But haven't Christians been praying this for thousands of years already? Why then are there still so many tears born of brutality and injustice? When will God's Kingdom *truly* come?

Well, it *has* come and it *is coming*. It has come in the truest sense because Jesus has come, died for the sins of the world, and been resurrected to begin the project of setting things right. It is certainly not completed, but it has begun and Jesus has invited us—his people—to participate.

Look at what Jesus says in Matthew 25:35-36, 40: "Whenever you give the hungry something to eat, the thirsty something to drink, the naked something to wear . . . you have done it for me" (my paraphrase). In other words, when we help others in need, we act on behalf of Jesus and the Kingdom of God. We give a glimpse of his presence in the world and make it a reality through our redemptive acts.

Can you help girls escape the sex trade in Cambodia? Maybe not. But you can help rebuild homes in New Orleans or assist in providing homes for the poor in your own city. You can pray for the family down the street in which the mother was just diagnosed with breast cancer. You can bring them dinner, mow their yard, walk their dog, and let them know they are not alone. You may not ever dig a well in Africa, but your small group can sponsor a refugee family in your city or volunteer at the local shelter for battered women.

You won't be able to solve all the world's problems, but you do have the capacity to help one child learn, help one widow care for her family, or care for one person who is sick. It's not rocket science, but it is the stuff of God's Kingdom.

WHAT DO YOU HAVE?

At this point you may feel a little overwhelmed. Or you may be taking inventory of people you can help, and how. You may be calculating how many hours per week you can afford to spare, or how much money you can contribute. This may awaken your inner techno-geek to start putting together spreadsheets and PowerPoint presentations for your Sunday school class. I know there are people out there like that; we have them in our church too.

Either way, I have one word for you: *Relax!*

Why do Christians have to make everything so complicated? Why does compassion have to become a project? It doesn't. And it shouldn't. At least it shouldn't start as a big, convoluted project. Just start with what you already have, what the Spirit of Christ has already grown in you—love, compassion, a heart of mercy, kindness. Cultivate and offer these things and see what Jesus does with them.

I love the scene in Mark 6 when Jesus miraculously feeds five thousand people. We're awestruck by the miracle, and rightly so, but we can easily miss something that is perhaps more important to our calling to participate in the compassionate work of Jesus.

When Jesus was told of the need, he didn't sit down with his disciples and strategize about what it would take to solve the problem. He simply asked them what they had to offer.

The answer: "Five [loaves], and two fishes" (Mark 6:38, KJV). And with that, Jesus worked the miracle.

Jesus did not ask his disciples to do the impossible. He asked only that they bring to him *what they had*. And that's all he asks from us. Just bring what you have. The miracle part is up to him.

And that's not to say that every encounter will be miraculous.

But when we show up with what we have, and don't worry about what we *don't* have, God's Spirit works through us to accomplish his purpose, whatever that might be.

So whether we are overwhelmed by the immensity of human suffering and need in our world, or just want to make one lesbian couple feel welcome at church, God doesn't ask us to give what we don't have. But he always uses what we are willing to give—love, compassion, time, a listening ear, a welcoming embrace.

We can work toward healing and alleviating suffering in Cambodia or in our neighborhood; we can be a friend to the hurting and give hope and help to those in need because this is the work of our King. The Jesus who calls us to feed the hungry, clothe the naked, and care for the sick is the same Jesus who says, "That work is my work. I am making all things new, and I have begun the process through you." Our motivation is that Christ has died to conquer both sin and death, Christ has risen to make all things new, and Christ will come again to bring to completion what he started.

Don't sit back and wait. Pray and work *now* for God's Kingdom to come *today*, in some small way, on earth as it is in heaven. Begin by prayerfully asking, "What can I do? What can we do?"

THY KINGDOM COME

Jesus himself teaches us to pray in a way that reflects our mission and calling to see the hope and healing of God's Kingdom become more of a reality on earth. We have heard and recited this prayer so many times, however, that we may miss the implications of what he is teaching us to ask.

> Our Father in heaven,
> hallowed be your name,
> your kingdom come,
> your will be done,
>   on earth as it is in heaven.
> Give us today our daily bread.
> And forgive us our debts,
>   as we also have forgiven our debtors.
> And lead us not into temptation,
>   but deliver us from the evil one.
>
> MATTHEW 6:9-13

The first thing we are to ask—before we ask for God's provision, forgiveness, and protection—is that his Kingdom would come down to earth.

Stop and think about that for a minute, especially in light of everything we have seen regarding the Resurrection and the meaning of our citizenship. Jesus is teaching us to say, "Father, let your Kingdom happen here. All you intend this world to be—all we think of as heaven—let that happen here. Not in some disembodied state up on a cloud somewhere, but *here*. And not just one day when we all die, but *now*."

This is nothing less than a prayer that everything discordant would be brought back into tune. It is decidedly *not* saying, "Father, help us to endure the disharmony and wait it all out until you get around to launching us off this god-forsaken rock." Rather, Jesus teaches us to ask God the Father to take all that has gone wrong with the world and make it right *here* and *now*, that our world, our cities, our neighborhoods—*today*—might be a little more like the Kingdom.

Friends, this is not philosophical speculation or theological conjecture. This is the story as God has told it—and he even gives us a glimpse of the end. His Kingdom *will* come—even more than it already has—and the reality of that hope should give us the courage to faithfully live and serve in the briarpatch today. God is not finished with this world. He has not abandoned it and will never forsake it—or us. He is committed not just to making it a tolerable place to live, but to making his dwelling here with us.

THE RIPTIDE

I have never been a huge fan of the ocean. My family is always astonished when we spend a few days at the beach and I show no desire to venture into the waves. Of course, I will go into the water to play with my kids, but I am perfectly content to sit in a chair, book in hand, watching them play with their cousins.

Some of my reluctance may be due to my past experience with the hazards and perils lurking offshore. I have felt the pinch of a crab on my toes and have been stung by never-seen jellyfish. Granted, crabs and jellyfish don't exactly constitute a death trap, but they are creatures I don't wish to encounter again.

A much more harrowing event happened when my wife

and I were newly married and went to the Atlantic coast of Florida with some friends. The waves were huge on this particular day, so a friend and I grabbed our boogie boards and waded into the churning water. After riding a wave almost all the way back to shore, I would turn around and swim back out to do it all over again, and again, and again.

I didn't always make it to shore. Some waves were too strong for my novice ability and would flip me over, drive me under, and skillfully shoot saltwater up my nose to power-wash my brain. During one particularly violent wipeout, I was separated from my board and slammed against the ocean floor before being tumbled head over heels. I couldn't tell which way was up, and I could feel myself being pulled by the water against my will, like the fat kid in Willy Wonka's chocolate river. I was out of breath and utterly helpless.

It was terrifying.

Eventually, the current released me, my head popped above the water, and I gulped at the fresh air. As I looked around, I was astonished at how far I was from the shore. I would never have gone that far out voluntarily, but I was just glad to be alive and in calm water.

That was my first—and only—experience with a riptide.

I have always known that every wave that comes to shore must go back out. What I didn't realize was how powerful, relentless, and dangerous that pull could be.

When we look at the world we live in—the world that God created—there is a relentless and destructive riptide at work as well. At the very beginning, God made the world in waves of beauty and harmony—humankind, the land, the animals, the heavens, and all the rest. Each wave was astonishing and wonderful and perfect. God himself pronounced every bit of it "good." And it *was* good—even perfect.

But then the riptide came, and it has been sucking stuff under ever since.

In Genesis 3, we see how profound and pervasive this riptide is. When Adam and Eve introduced sin into the world, it messed everything up, pulling against God's intentions. It created alienation between God and humanity. It created alienation between the sexes. It created alienation between humanity and creation. Our work is cursed. The harmony that should exist between us and nature is now fraught with tension. What should be a source of life now brings frustration.

The riptide also created alienation within people's hearts and between us and our fellow human beings. There is now shame and a desire to hide—to cover our nakedness. Rather than being transparent, we want to control what others know of us. Not only do we dislike what we are on the inside, but we seek to hide what we are on the outside as well. In short, the riptide of sin has taken every facet of our humanity and our world and pulled it out of joint. This is not the way things are supposed to be.

But the riptide is not the final word. God has no intention of letting the riptide win. The current of his redemptive purpose is far more powerful.

THE NEW HEAVENS AND NEW EARTH
The book of Revelation is a God-given vision of "the end," except it's not really the end; it's a new beginning, a time

when peace and harmony will be restored, the riptide will be removed, and the Kingdom of Heaven will come fully and finally to earth. It really will be quite extraordinary.

> Then I saw a new heaven and a new earth, for the
> old heaven and the old earth had disappeared.
> And the sea was also gone. And I saw the holy city,
> the new Jerusalem, coming down from God out
> of heaven like a bride beautifully dressed for her
> husband.
>
> I heard a loud shout from the throne, saying,
> "Look, God's home is now among his people! He
> will live with them, and they will be his people. God
> himself will be with them. He will wipe every tear
> from their eyes, and there will be no more death or
> sorrow or crying or pain. All these things are gone
> forever."
>
> And the one sitting on the throne said, "Look,
> I am making everything new!"
>
> REVELATION 21:1-5, NLT

"Look, I am making everything new" does not mean, "Watch while I chuck all this mess into the celestial trash can and start over from scratch with something entirely different." No, "making everything new" is the language of redemption, reconciliation, restoration, and transformation. What we know now as "heaven and earth" will pass away—they will be transformed and renewed so thoroughly and completely that the fractured and splintered existence we now endure will no longer exist. The riptide will be forever washed away by the water of life (Revelation 22:1-3).

In the Bible, Jerusalem is the primary center of God's activity on earth. The Temple in Jerusalem represented God's presence in the world. What the Temple did in part—as the place of worship, prayer, and atonement for sin through sacrifice—Jesus expanded beyond a single physical place. The new Jerusalem represents the consummation of the harmonious and intimate trajectory between God and his people that began in the Garden of Eden. Now God will bring his plan to full fruition as his presence literally comes to earth, and heaven and earth become one.

This transforms our view of what heaven is. And it means that what we do now on earth matters. How we love matters. How we serve matters. Our joy, forgiveness, and compassion matter. Our efforts to bring wholeness to shattered lives through reconciliation and healing matter. Our worship matters. It all matters.

We are called to practice now what will become an ever-present reality when the earth is finally restored. As Christians, we embody God's healing presence. (That's why we're called the body of Christ.) We are ambassadors of his grace and mercy.

As we pray for God to make his Kingdom a reality now, we are to work for all that is holy, just, right, and pure; and we are to stand against all that is corrupt, unjust, and defiled. That's what life in the briarpatch is all about. We do all this in anticipation of the day when God will come and literally make his dwelling place on earth.

As we enter the briarpatch of our tangled, fallen world, we take the presence of Jesus with us, and we find that he is already there, in the midst of the thorns and thistles, preparing the way for restoration, reconciliation, and redemption.

ACKNOWLEDGMENTS

Wes Yoder is one of the kindest and wisest people I have ever met. He also happens to be a very talented agent, and I am privileged to call him my friend. His guidance, prayer, and encouragement through the bewildering business of publishing has been a comforting and trustworthy light. As Wes encouraged me to honor Christ, he helped me become a better writer as well.

At Tyndale, Jan Long Harris and Sarah Atkinson: what can I say? It seems we began laughing from the first moment we met and have not stopped since! I will be forever grateful for your taking a chance on an obscure pastor from the trailer park who thought he might write a book. They invited me into the Tyndale family and have guided me with impressive competence and care. Dave Lindstedt, my editor, has a brutal and brilliant red pen. He often seemed to understand what I really wanted to say more than I did myself. In many ways, he deserves a coauthor credit—but none of the blame for my mistakes, of course. Sharon Leavitt takes such wonderful care of the Tyndale authors and has always been eager to answer questions and give much-needed encouragement. The mention of just a few does not negate my profound respect, admiration, and gratitude for the entire Tyndale team.

Then there is Jessica Quinn, who always seems to have the energy and excitement of a child on Christmas morning—ever something new to discover and explore. Her simple words, "Have you ever thought of writing a book? Others need to hear these stories," and her knowledge of the publishing industry were catalysts to this very long process. Her encouragement has been unwavering as she doggedly read the earliest manuscript and championed this book to any who would listen.

Thank you to my church family at All Souls, for having the courage to go with me into the briarpatch. This is your story. Thank you for allowing me the privilege of being your pastor and granting me time away in the summer of 2011 to rest and write.

There would be no book without quiet and creative places to write. These were provided by generous friends who opened up their homes to me and my family while we were on sabbatical. Thank you to Chris and Nancy Gerlach, Bruce and Missy Terrell, Kermit and Cheryl Horn, and Jim Wilkinson.

I am grateful to Chris and Katie Torres, Michael Dunaway, Josh Jackson, Matt Christian, and Tuck Bartholomew, for being so eager to help in big and small ways. Whether giving insight to the manuscript, taking a picture, or helping me make necessary connections, they were always ready and willing to assist.

I am indebted to Scot Sherman, my mentor and friend, for helping me dare to dream that the church could be more.

On this earth, my story begins and ends with my family, particularly my wife, Carrie. It is no exaggeration to say that this book would never have been more than a fleeting thought were it not for her kind and consistent encouragement for me to "just start writing." Calvin, Emma, and Audrey are three of my very favorite people in the world. They remind me to laugh, teach me to love, and stretch me to become a better person. I am truly honored to be their father. Throughout the writing of this book, whether on sabbatical or vacation, in the evenings after dinner or on the weekends, my family never complained when I had to escape in order to write. Their sacrifice has been as great as mine.

DISCUSSION GUIDE

CHAPTER 1
YOU ARE HERE:
COMING TO GRIPS WITH OUR FEAR

1. What did Shayne learn about life and faith from his conversation with Ilya? Describe a conversation you've had in which Jesus felt especially present and alive to you.

2. What does the author mean when he uses the phrase "life in the briarpatch"? Describe what this looks like in your own life and in your church.

3. What does Jesus' time on earth, including his death and resurrection, say about the briarpatch?

CHAPTER 2
WE'RE NOT IN KANSAS ANYMORE:
CLEARING THE LAND MINES

1. What are some cultural and ecclesiastical land mines mentioned in the chapter? How do these compare to the land mines you see around you? How can we defuse the land mines in our lives?

2. What attracted Brian to the church? How does this compare to the culture and climate in your own church? How

can you make room for people to connect before they commit?

3. How do we make room in our lives for people who are different from us? What specific steps can you take to make room in your life, your family's life, and the life of the church?

4. How does the language you use to describe your relationship with God create open doors for others? How does it create barriers? How can you turn those barriers into open doors?

CHAPTER 3
THE WAY IN: NAVIGATING THE THICKET

1. Do you feel as if you have to choose between superficial/safe friendships or downplaying/hiding your faith? Which do you tend toward more often and why? What is a better option?

2. How is love "the way in"? What stands out to you in 1 John 4:7-12?

3. In what ways have you separated your spiritual and physical lives? What can you do to live with greater integrity in the sanctuary and on the street?

CHAPTER 4
THE ICEBERG LURKS: DANGER BENEATH THE SURFACE

1. How is your heart like an iceberg? What issues do you hide beneath the surface?

2. When Jesus met the woman at the well, he saw through her brokenness and offered her healing in the form of "living water." Put yourself in her place. If you met Jesus under similar circumstances, what brokenness would he see in your heart? How can you begin to open yourself up to his "living water"?

3. What does it mean to live in the power of Christ's resurrection?

CHAPTER 5
VERTIGO: THE DANCE OF DOUBT AND FAITH

1. Why is doubt a "dirty little secret" that many Christians don't want to talk about? How does the author suggest we should deal with our doubt?

2. In order to believe in God and love him, we need some "objective, foundational evidence that he exists and that what he says is true." What pieces of foundational evidence have you based your faith on?

3. What mysteries do you experience in life? How is your relationship with God a mystery? How have you reconciled the mystery of God with your need for evidence?

4. How would you respond to the author's suggestion that "we should engage in worshiping God even if we're not sure we believe in him"? How do you worship God in your own life?

CHAPTER 6
PIRATES AND FREAKS: HAVING THE COURAGE TO CHANGE

1. How have you seen the totem poles of piety and cultural popularity dictate people's behavior? Is there a difference between the totem poles in secular settings versus Christian settings?

2. What does the author say is the reason we fear admitting our imperfections and failures? Do you agree with him? How can we be healed from the fear of being exposed?

3. Describe a time when you were "undressed" by God. How did this lead to healing and growth in your life? Or did it?

4. How can you apply the parable of the Lost Sheep in your everyday life? How does it affect your attitude and approach to "*real* sinners"?

CHAPTER 7
FOLLOWING THE STORY: CAN SUCH AN OLD BOOK EVER LEAD THE WAY?

1. In what ways is "the story of the Bible foundationally one of hope"?

2. Do you trust the Bible? Are there parts that seem confusing or contradictory to you? How do you reconcile those parts with the Bible's claim that it is the revelation of God?

3. Why do you suppose God allowed the Bible to contain so much "crazy stuff"? How does this support or undermine your faith in God's Word?

4. Discuss the difference between viewing the Bible as a compilation of propositional summaries and theological proofs or as a complex, interwoven story of a God who loves, and is redeeming, the world. How can these viewpoints be reconciled?

CHAPTER 8
MOVING TOWARD THE RUBBLE: MEETING GOD IN HURRICANES AND THE HOMELESS

1. Describe Shayne's friendship with Mr. Buford. Have you ever had a friendship with someone whose perspective is so different from your own? How has this relationship affected you? What have you done to preserve the relationship and keep the dialogue open?

2. As Christians, we are called to be discerning, but we are also called to be loving and caring toward the people around us. How do we balance the two?

3. We tend to think of fasting as going without food for an extended period. How does the prophet Isaiah describe the kind of fast that God desires (see Isaiah 58)?

4. In what ways can you "move toward the rubble" in your neighborhood, community, or town? How does that align with your understanding of evangelism?

CHAPTER 9
MISSING PIECES: FINDING THE MEANING OF JESUS IN THE CRUCIBLE OF SUFFERING

1. What do you think of the quotes at the beginning of this chapter? Do you agree with them? When have you seen them as true or untrue in your life?

2. What explanations do people give for why there is evil and suffering in our world? What answer would you give?

3. How does God use pain and suffering in our lives to further his redemptive purpose for the world? How has your own suffering uniquely equipped you to offer "empathy amid the thorns" to someone else?

CHAPTER 10
LOOKING FOR THE RAINBOW: DOES GOD REALLY HATE GAYS?

1. Describe your own experience with the issue of homosexuality and the church. How has the church typically responded to this issue?

2. Describe the "chameleon" and "musk ox" responses people or churches often have in regard to difficult social and cultural issues. Which response do you tend toward? What is the third way?

3. What do you think causes the church to respond to issues of sexuality differently than it does to other sensitive issues? What does loving the sinner and hating the sin really look like in our world today? How can we

be accepting of people without being accepting of their sin, especially when it comes to a sinful lifestyle?

4. What would it mean for you to go "all in" to the briarpatches in your life? What would need to change, and what would stay the same?

CHAPTER 11

OPEN BORDERS: LIVING OUTSIDE THE WALLS

1. In what ways are you already in the midst of the briarpatch? How can you model the hope and healing of the gospel of Jesus Christ right where you are?

2. How does faith in Jesus differ from adherence to other religions?

3. In what ways do you need to "get out of Tennessee"? How can you and your church become more intentional about doing this? What are the benefits of living with "open borders"?

4. What are some of the "subconscious signals we transmit that subtly undermine the simple and free invitation of Jesus"? In what ways are we making things more complicated than Jesus himself did? How can we become a more accurate reflection of God's grace?

CHAPTER 12

GETTING IN TUNE: THE HARMONY OF HEAVEN AND EARTH

1. The author says that Jesus' purpose was "not so much to get us into heaven as it was to get heaven into us and into the world." What do you think about this

perspective? How have you seen God's Kingdom here on earth already?

2. What do you have that can be offered to God for him to do the miraculous with? Are you willing to give them to God and let him work?

3. Identify a briarpatch in your own life or community. What would it take for you to personally enter it, and how would it change you, your church, and the people God has placed around you?

4. How does understanding the book of Revelation as a new beginning, rather than as an end, affect your perspective on living your life today?

NOTES

CHAPTER 1: YOU ARE HERE

1. J. K. Rowling, *Harry Potter and the Prisoner of Azkaban* (New York: Scholastic, 1999), 187, 247.
2. Eric Bazilian, "One of Us," recorded 1995.
3. James Davison Hunter, *To Change the World* (New York: Oxford University Press, 2010), 193.

CHAPTER 2: WE'RE NOT IN KANSAS ANYMORE

1. Timothy Keller, "Post-Everythings," *byFaith* magazine 1, no. 1 (June/July 2003), 29–30. Reprinted by Westminster Theological Resources, http://www.wts.edu/resources/articles/keller_posteverythings.html.
2. I believe that celebrating the Lord's Supper is the most evangelistic moment in the corporate worship of God. It is that moment when all followers of Jesus are called to remember their identity as the daughters and sons of God—that they belong at the family table of their Father. Likewise, it is a time when those who are not yet followers of Jesus are clearly reminded that they are on the outside looking in —that they, in fact, do not have something that all these other people have. In our church, everyone comes forward to receive the bread and wine. But before they come forward, we remind them to consider their standing in Christ. We say, "If you are not a follower of Jesus, this is not your meal and we ask that you not participate, because according to Scripture (1 Corinthians 11:26), by participating in this meal you proclaim the Lord's death until he returns. You are declaring that the life, death, and resurrection of Christ are a reality in your life, and we would not want you to proclaim something that is not true. But we are glad you are here, and we want you to keep coming, keep doubting, keep questioning. You are welcome here and we look forward to the day when you do give your life to Christ and join us in this meal."
3. Alice Ambrose, ed., *Wittgenstein's Lectures, Cambridge, 1932–1935* (Amherst, NY: Prometheus, 2001), 30.

CHAPTER 3: THE WAY IN

1. Dietrich Bonhoeffer, *Ethics* (New York: Touchstone, 1995), 57–58.
2. John 17:15, 18.

CHAPTER 4: THE ICEBERG LURKS

1. G. William Domhoff, "Wealth, Income, and Power," *Who Rules America?* last modified March 2012, http://www2.ucsc.edu/whorulesamerica/power /wealth.html.
2. Christian Smith and Michael O. Emerson, with Patricia Snell, *Passing the Plate: Why American Christians Don't Give Away More Money* (New York: Oxford University, 2008), 33–39.
3. "Statistics on Pornography, Sexual Addiction, and Online Perpetrators," *SafeFamilies*, http://www.safefamilies.org/sfStats.php.
4. Audrey Barrick, "Porn Addiction Flooding Culture, Church," *Christianity Today* (June 6, 2007), http://www.christiantoday.com/article/porn .addiction.flooding.culture.church/11029.htm.
5. According to the Nielsen Company, 29 percent of working adults accessed pornography at work during the month of March 2010; http://www .cbsnews.com/8301-503544_162-20003319-503544.html.

CHAPTER 5: VERTIGO

1. Mother Teresa, *Come Be My Light: The Private Writings of the Saint of Calcutta* (New York: Doubleday Religion, 2007), 192–193.
2. Ibid., 288.
3. Konstantin Mochulsky, *Dostoevsky: His Life and Work,* trans. Michael A. Minihan (Princeton, NJ: Princeton University Press, 1967), 650.
4. Timothy Keller, *The Reason for God: Belief in an Age of Skepticism* (New York: Dutton, 2008), xvi–xvii.
5. N. T. Wright, *Who Was Jesus?* (London: SPCK, 1992), 63.
6. For a discussion about examining our doubts, see Timothy Keller, *The Reason for God*, xvi–xix.
7. Philip James Bailey, *Festus* (London: William Pickering, 1852), 47.
8. Keller, *The Reason for God*, xvii.
9. Ibid.
10. G. K. Chesterton, *What's Wrong with the World?* (London: Cassell, 1910), 39.

CHAPTER 6: PIRATES AND FREAKS

1. C. S. Lewis, *The Voyage of the "Dawn Treader"* (New York: HarperTrophy, 1980), 115–116, 120.

CHAPTER 7: FOLLOWING THE STORY

1. Charles Dickens, *Great Expectations* (San Francisco: Ignatius, 2010), 71–72.

2. Ibid., 73.
3. Ibid., 75.
4. C. S. Lewis, "Modern Theology and Biblical Criticism," in *Christian Reflections* (Grand Rapids: Eerdmans, 1995), 155.

CHAPTER 8: MOVING TOWARD THE RUBBLE
1. Ray Cannata, personal correspondence with the author.

CHAPTER 9: MISSING PIECES
1. Jean-Paul Sartre, *Basic Writings*, trans. Philip Mairet (New York: Routledge, 2001), 32.

CHAPTER 10: LOOKING FOR THE RAINBOW
1. Aleksandr I. Solzhenitsyn, *The Gulag Archipelago Volume 1: An Experiment in Literary Investigation* (New York: HarperCollins, 1991), 168; italics added.
2. This first section is adapted from an essay of mine, "The Fracture in Our Soul," in David Kinnaman and Gabe Lyons, *UnChristian* (Grand Rapids: Baker, 2007), 110–111.
3. Kinnaman and Lyons, *UnChristian*, 93.
4. Ibid., 97–98.
5. Dick Keyes, *Chameleon Christianity* (Eugene, OR: Wipf and Stock, 2003), 23–51.

CHAPTER 11: OPEN BORDERS
1. John 14:6, NLT
2. G. K. Chesterton, *Orthodoxy* (Chicago: Moody, 2009), 52.
3. C. S. Lewis, "What Are We to Make of Jesus Christ?" in *God in the Dock: Essays on Theology and Ethics* (Grand Rapids: Eerdmans, 1970), 157–158.
4. Lesslie Newbigin, *The Gospel in a Pluralist Society* (Grand Rapids: Eerdmans, 1989), 159; italics added.

CHAPTER 12: GETTING IN TUNE
1. N. T. Wright, *Surprised by Hope: Rethinking Heaven, the Resurrection, and the Mission of the Church* (New York: HarperOne, 2008), 209.
2. From the *NGO Statement to the 2001 Consultative Group Meeting on Cambodia*: "Child prostitution and child trafficking have become grave problems in Cambodia. In Phnom Penh, there are an estimated 10,000–15,000 child prostitutes." Cited by Thomas M. Steinfatt in "Measuring the Number of Trafficked Women and Children in Cambodia: A Direct Observation Field Study, Part 3 of a Series," page 2, http://preventhumantrafficking.org/storage/article-downloads/MeasuringTheNumber3.pdf.

ABOUT THE AUTHOR

SHAYNE WHEELER is the founding pastor of All Souls Fellowship in Decatur, Georgia, an eclectic and funky church about five miles east of downtown Atlanta. Prior to starting All Souls, Shayne served churches in Missouri, Virginia, and the suburbs of Atlanta. Before he became a professional Christian, he was a shoe salesman, mattress mover, warehouse worker, and waiter. He met his wife, Carrie, at Western Kentucky University, and she quickly became his best friend. They married in 1992 and share a very noisy home with their three busy kids and two handsome dogs. In his free time, Shayne enjoys exercising, traveling with his family, riding motorcycles, and reading quietly on his awesome front porch. He holds a BA in philosophy and religion from Western Kentucky University and an MDiv from Covenant Theological Seminary.

Online Discussion *guide*

TAKE *your* TYNDALE READING EXPERIENCE *to the* NEXT LEVEL

A FREE discussion guide for this book is available at bookclubhub.net, perfect for sparking conversations in your book group or for digging deeper into the text on your own.

www.bookclubhub.net

You'll also find free discussion guides for other Tyndale books, e-newsletters, e-mail devotionals, virtual book tours, and more!

"Is this what Jesus told you guys to do?"

Light shows, fog machines, worship bands, offering plates—Is this what Jesus intended? **Atheist Matt Casper wants to know.**

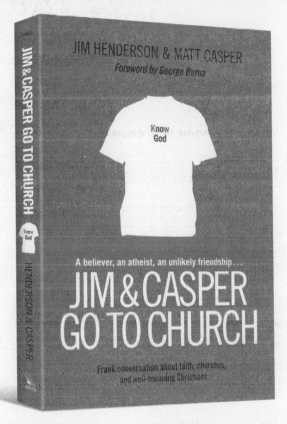

Longtime Christian Jim Henderson realized that he had no idea how a nonbeliever might interpret a usual Sunday service . . . or what might inspire him or her to come back.

So he decided to ask! Jim invited an atheist—Matt Casper—to visit twelve leading churches with him and give the "first impression" perspective of a nonbeliever. Follow along with Jim and Casper on their visits, and eavesdrop as they discuss what they found. Their articulate, sometimes humorous, and always insightful dialogue offers Christians a view of an environment where we've become overly comfortable: the church.

ISBN 978-1-4143-5858-1